An Invisible Minority

THE NEW IMMIGRANTS SERIES

Allyn & Bacon

Series Editor, Nancy Foner, State University of New York at Purchase

An Invisible Minority: Brazilians in New York City

Maxine L. Margolis
University of Florida

Allyn and Bacon

Boston • London • Toronto • Sydney • Tokyo • Singapore

Series Editor: Sarah L. Dunbar
Vice President, Social Science: Karen Hanson
Series Editorial Assistant: Elissa V. Schaen
Marketing Manager: Karon Bowers
Consulting Editor: Sylvia Shepard
Manufacturing Buyer: Suzanne Lareau
Cover Administrator: Suzanne Harbison
Cover Designer: Jenny Hart
Editorial-Production Service: Omegatype Typography, Inc.

ISBN: 0-205-26687-8

Printed in the United States of America
10 9 8 7 6 5 4 3 2 1   02 01 00 99 98 97

All photos are credited to J. T. Milanich

Contents

Foreword to the Series

The United States is now experiencing the largest wave of immigration in the country's history. The 1990s, it is predicted, will see more new immigrants enter the United States than in any decade in American history. New immigrants from Asia, Latin America, and the Caribbean are changing the American ethnic landscape.

Until recently, immigration was associated in the minds of many Americans with the massive influx of southern and eastern Europeans at the turn of the century. Since the late 1960s, America has again become a country of large-scale immigration, this time attracting newcomers from developing societies of the world. The number of foreign-born is at an all-time high: nearly 20 million foreign-born persons were counted in the 1990 census. Although immigrants are a smaller share of the nation's population than they were earlier in the century—8 percent in 1990 compared to about 15 percent in 1910—recent immigrants are having an especially dramatic impact because their geographic concentration is greater today. About half of all immigrants entering the United Sates during the 1980s moved to eight urban areas: Los Angeles, New York, Miami, Anaheim, Chicago, Washington, D.C., Houston, and San Francisco. America's major urban centers are, increasingly, immigrant cities with new ethnic mixes.

Who are the new immigrants? What are their lives like here? How are they redefining themselves and their cultures? And how are they contributing to a new and changing America? The *New Immigrant Series* provides a set of case studies that explores these themes among a variety of new immigrant groups. Each book in the series is written by a recognized expert who has done extensive in-depth ethnographic research on one of the immigrant groups. The groups represent a broad range of today's arrivals, coming from a variety of countries and cultures. The studies, based on research done in different parts of the country, cover a wide geographical range from New York to California.

Most of the books in the series are written by anthropologists. All draw on qualitative research that shows what it means to be an immigrant in America today. As part of each study, individual immigrants tell their stories, which will help give a sense of the experiences and problems of the newcomers. Through the case studies, a dynamic picture emerges of the way immigrants are carving out new lives for themselves at the same time as they are creating a new and more diverse America.

The ethnographic case study, long the anthropologist's trademark, provides a depth often lacking in research on immigrants in the United States. Moreover, many anthropologists, like a number of authors in the *New Immigrants Series,* have done research in the sending society as well as in the United States. Having field experience at both ends of the migration chain makes anthropologists particularly sensitive to the role of transnational ties that link immigrants to their home societies. With firsthand experience of immigrants in their home culture, anthropologists are also well-positioned to appreciate continuities as well as changes in the immigrant setting.

As the United States faces a growing backlash against immigration, and many Americans express ambivalence and sometimes hostility toward the latest arrivals, it becomes more important than ever to learn about the new immigrants and to hear their voices. The case studies in the *New Immigrants Series* will help readers understand the cultures and lives of the newest Americans and bring out the complex ways the newcomers are coming to terms with and creatively adapting to life in a new land.

NANCY FONER
Series Editor

Preface

WHAT CAN WE LEARN
FROM BRAZILIAN IMMIGRATION?

Brazilian immigrants in New York City are the focus of this book. But it is about more than one particular immigrant group because the story of Brazilians illustrates many of the debates that surround immigration to the United States:

- Who are the new immigrants and what attracts them to this country?

- What kind of jobs do they hold and what niche do immigrants fill in the American economy?

- Are they taking jobs away from native-born workers?

- Why the recent outcry against immigration to the U.S?

- What about the hot button issue of illegal immigration?

- Do all undocumented immigrants fit the standard stereotype of unschooled peasants fleeing poverty and lives of desperation?

While this book is about Brazilian immigrants, it is also an account of undocumented immigration; about half of the Brazilians I met in New York were undocumented at the time of my study. And so, questions related to this controversial issue became one of my research interests. I wanted to know how Brazilians became undocumented, how they secured visas to come to the United States, how they entered the country, and what it was like to live "out of status," that is, as an immigrant who is working in this country illegally. But it is important to emphasize in the strongest terms possible that *nothing* I relate in the pages to follow is unique to Brazilians. Brazilians represent undocumented immigrants of diverse national origins. As such, they serve as surrogates for many other "out of status" immigrant groups with powerful economic motives for living in this country.

We will also see that this is a tale that contradicts the prevailing American stereotype of the "illegal alien"[1] as a young, uneducated male who comes from an impoverished village in rural Mexico. From the earliest days of my research in New York City, I realized that the Brazilian immigrants I was interviewing had little in common with the exemplary "illegal" of contemporary American discourse. Most of the Brazilians seeking their fortune in this country are middle and lower-middle class and many have university educations. And so, this also became a narrative about a new kind of immigrant, an immigrant who was not fleeing from dire poverty or political repression. Rather, Brazilians—like many immigrants now arriving in this country—are economic refugees escaping their nation's chaotic economy. Moreover, they claim to be sojourners not settlers; immigrants who are in this country temporarily, visitors who will only stay long enough to save money to be used after the return home.

The Brazilian immigrant experience bears many parallels to that of other immigrant groups, but it is also uniquely their own. Throughout this book I will describe features of Brazilian society that help decipher the culture clashes and stresses and strains that particularly mark the Brazilian encounter with immigrant status. Here I have drawn on my own familiarity with Brazilian culture and my extensive experience doing field work in Brazil and among Brazilian immigrants in Paraguay.

HOW THIS RESEARCH WAS DONE

The research for this book was done in two phases. During the first phase, which lasted several weeks, I did an informal survey and open-ended interviews with about fifty Brazilians, including both recent immigrants and long-term residents of New York.

---

1. Because it has become an incendiary epithet, I have generally avoided using the phrase "illegal alien" throughout this book and have used "undocumented immigrant" or "immigrant without papers" instead.

Through these interviews I became familiar with the general contours of Brazilian immigration to the city, its history, the neighborhoods in which Brazilians live, and the kind of jobs they hold. I then drew up a series of questions that I wanted to answer in my research.

I gathered most of my data during phase two, a twelve month period in the early 1990s when I lived in New York City while on sabbatical from the University of Florida. First, I selected informants and filled out one hundred questionnaires for a sample of them. The questionnaires covered most aspects of Brazilian immigrant life, from the decision to migrate to New York to their subsequent experiences working and living in the city. A series of questions were meant to profile the immigrants—their vital statistics, hometowns, social and educational background and prior work histories.

Choosing the subjects for these questionnaires became a major dilemma because, for obvious reasons, it is extremely difficult to estimate the size of populations that are partly composed of undocumented immigrants (Cornelius 1982). This was certainly true of Brazilians in New York City. A majority of Brazilians did not participate in the 1990 United States Census and no other quantitative data is available on them. As a result, the number of Brazilians residing in New York City is unknown, as is their residential distribution within the metropolitan area. Thus, there is no sampling frame for selecting individuals from this population, making it impossible to come up with a random sample of Brazilian immigrants in the city.

Snowball sampling, a non-random sampling technique, was used instead because it has proved to be useful in contacting "hidden" populations, like undocumented immigrants (Cornelius; Bernard 1994). Snowball sampling uses informants' own networks of friends and relatives to create a sample. I used it in the following way: After making initial contacts with a few Brazilian immigrants, I asked each one for the names of one or two other Brazilians who might agree to be interviewed. These, in turn, were asked for additional names; the process continued, and a network of informants was created.

The drawback of snowball sampling is that the data gathered cannot be generalized beyond the sample at hand. In other words, the statistical portait of Brazilians presented in this book should be seen only as a useful guide because the sample on which it is based was not drawn randomly. However, keeping these limitations in mind, snowball sampling can still be a very credible research tool when combined with qualitative ethnographic techniques.

Aside from the subjects of the questionnaires, I had informal conversations with dozens and dozens of other Brazilians—more than 250 in all—doing what anthropologists call "participant observation." During both phases of the research, I visited peoples' homes and attended concerts and sporting events. I went to church services and street fairs, and spent time at stores, restaurants, and nightclubs frequented by Brazilians. I even visited some Brazilians at work. In short, I tried to immerse myself in the daily life of New York's Brazilian immigrant community.

I also spent three weeks in Brazil in which I interviewed officials of the American Consulate in Rio de Janeiro and some returned migrants. I traveled to the city of Governador Valadares in Minas Gerais state, a major exporter of *brazucas,* as Brazilians living in the United States are called. I talked to a few dozen people there—local officials, travel agents, families with relatives in the United States—and collected data on the history and impact of the emigrant flow. Insights and data from my stay in Brazil appear throughout the book.

Finally, I have tried to generalize about the Brazilian immigrant experience in the United States by visiting Brazilian communities in Boston and Newark and by talking with immigrants and community leaders there. I have also included the findings of other researchers in these communities. All of this information is incorporated in the present book which is an abbreviated, updated version of an earlier study (Margolis 1994).

Acknowledgements

Several people contributed to this book. The research and insights of Ana Cristina Braga Martes on Brazilians in Boston gave me an invaluable comparative perspective on Brazilian immigration to the United States. She was also a lively and instructive guide to the Brazilian community in the Boston area. I also learned a great deal in an informal conversation with Roberto Lima and Bispo Filho, editors of the *Brazilian Voice* published in Newark. Many dozens of Brazilians in New York helped me with my initial research and generously shared their experiences as immigrants with me. I want to single out Gisele Fontes Da Rocha for her assistance in my more recent endeavors and also thank my economists-in-residence, Nicola Cetorelli and Michele Gambera, for their Internet-mediated assistance finding data on the Brazilian economy. I also appreciate Nancy Foner's careful editing and useful suggestions for improving this work. And, as always, I am deeply grateful to JTM not only for his help with photo selection and editing but also for his TLC while I was writing this book.

An Invisible Minority

New Ingredient in the Melting Pot

In July 1994 televisions sets all over Brazil were tuned to the new evening soap opera *Patria Minha* ("My Homeland"), a saga of a Brazilian family that had emigrated to New York City. The program's first episode introduced viewers to Pedro and Esther as they struggled with the decision to remain in the United States—where they had lived for eight years—or return to Brazil. At about the same time a study of the Brazilian census revealed that between 1980 and 1990 one million Brazilians had vanished from the nation—presumably lost to emigration, and the Brazilian government launched a campaign to encourage immigrants to return to their homeland. The theme of Brazilians abroad was echoed in stories in the nation's most widely read newsmagazines which proclaimed that there was a "Brazilian Exodus" and gave details of the "Brazilian Diaspora" (Corrêa 1994; Lucena 1996; Bustos 1995).

But what is happening here? After all, when Americans picture immigrants in New York City or other parts of the United States they are likely to think of Mexicans, Haitians, Cubans and Central Americans or even Koreans or Indians. But Brazilians? Most Americans associate Brazil with tropical forests, World Cup soccer, *bossa nova* music and sunny beaches awash with bronzed, scantily clad bathers, but certainly not with immigrants to this country. But the fact is that beginning in the 1980s as the Brazilian economy went into a tailspin, untold numbers of Brazilians migrated to the United States, Canada, various countries in Europe,

Japan and Australia. Yet it is also true that until quite recently Brazilians did not think of themselves as immigrants because they had had no experience with emigration. As one Brazilian put it: "We have not been immigrants since the Portuguese discovered Brazil in 1500. They discovered it and then they just sat there."

PIONEER MIGRATION

Scattered enclaves of Brazilians have long existed in the United States. It is unclear where Brazil's pioneer immigrants to the United States first settled, but already by the mid- and late 1960s, there were small Brazilian communities in New York City, the Catskill Mountain region of New York State, Newark, New Jersey, Boston, and California. Some of the first Brazilian immigrants to arrive in the United States came from Governador Valadares, a city of some 230,000 in the state of Minas Gerais in south central Brazil. Valadarenses—as natives of the city are called—still make up a major segment of the Brazilian population in the Boston area, Newark and in some towns in Connecticut and south Florida. In fact, immigrants from various parts of Minas Gerais are well represented in Brazilian communities throughout the United States.

GOVERNADOR VALADARES: A SENDING COMMUNITY

An interesting question is why such a disproportionate share of Brazil's pioneer immigrants come from a single city in the interior of Brazil. Why has Governador Valadares become an immigrant sending community with perhaps 45,000 of its citizens living in the United States, a place whose sons and daughters send an estimated 12 million dollars a month in remittance money to relatives back home (De Souza 1996)?

While large scale emigration from Governador Valadares only began around 1980, it has deeper roots that can be traced back to World War II. It was then that the long period of contact between the city and the United States began. During the war, Brazil became the world's leading producer of mica, at that time a critical material for insulation. Mica was mined in the state of Minas Gerais, with the major mining and processing centers located in and around Governador Valadares. After the war the industry faded, but the stage had been set for future emigration from the city because mica was responsible for the American presence there. Americans were associated with various aspects of the industry, while other Americans came to the city to work with Brazil's national public health service. Because of the city's role as a mining center for materials needed in the war effort, a public health office was set up to combat malaria. Both public health concerns and the mica industry brought American medical personnel and engineers to town, and some hired Valadarenses as household servants.

Local tradition has it that when these Americans were living in Governador Valadares they often paid with dollar bills—for shoeshines, taxi rides, sandwiches—and rarely asked for change. Since in those days the equivalent of a dollar bill in Brazilian currency was quite a lot of money, townspeople became convinced that, as the saying goes, money must grow on trees in the United States. This is why, when the Americans returned home after the war and invited some of their local employees to go with them, the invitations were readily accepted. Such is the tale of how emigrants from Governador Valadares first came to the United States (Margolis 1990).

Today a culture of out-migration exists in Governador Valadares and the surrounding towns, a culture found in communities that have extensive, long established patterns of international migration; children in them grow up expecting to migrate as part of their life experience. As such, many young Valadarenses plan to migrate to the United States instead of working on the family farm or going on to college. And so the continued draw of dollars and the long tradition of emigration have made Governador Valadares the "emigrant capital of Brazil." So many townspeople now live in the United States, according to a local joke, that only the mayor has stayed behind to turn out the lights when he leaves (Margolis 1990).

The small pioneer enclaves of Valadarenses and other Brazilians remained relatively unknown in Brazil and received virtually no news coverage there. During the 1970s and early 1980s the rate of immigration from Brazil began a slow but steady increase; then from the mid-1980s to the end of the decade it soared. Tens of thousands of Brazilians headed for New York, New Jersey, Massachusetts, Florida, and California and these same states remain the primary areas of Brazilian residence in the United States today. They are home to perhaps two-thirds of the Brazilians currently living in this country. Smaller Brazilian enclaves are found

Two young girls looking in a shop window in Governador
Valadares. In communities with a culture of out-migration, young
people grow up expecting to migrate abroad.

in Chicago, Philadelphia, Washington, DC, Roanoke, Virginia,
and in Houston and Austin, Texas.

In terms of sheer numbers, the greater New York metropolitan
area probably has the largest Brazilian population in the United
States. Aside from New York City itself, a number of Brazilian nuclei dot the region. Brazilians live in Westchester, a suburban
county just north of the city and in the town of Mineola on Long
Island. The city of Newark, long a center of Portuguese immigration, is also now home to a sizeable Brazilian community, as are
the Connecticut towns of Danbury, Waterbury and Bridgeport.

Boston, including its suburbs and the communities south and
west of the city, is second only to New York as a site of Brazilian
immigration. In some communities in the region the Brazilian
presence cannot be overlooked. To cite just one example: in the
town of Marlboro just west of Boston, Brazilians account for nearly one quarter of the local population.

Moving away from the northeast, central and southern Florida are also nuclei of Brazilian settlement and some call the small
community of Pompano Beach the "Brazilian immigrant capital
of south Florida." And on the west coast, Los Angeles, San Diego
and especially San Francisco have burgeoning Brazilian enclaves.

BRAZILIANS IN GOTHAM

If you were to visit New York City and ask any native New Yorker how to get to Little Italy or Chinatown, you would be quickly directed to take the subway or a taxi downtown to either of these well known tourist sites. But were you to inquire how to get to Little Brazil you would be met with a puzzled look. "Little Brazil? What's that?" would be the response. The reason for the puzzled look is that New York has no distinct Brazilian residential neighborhood, no area that is comparable to Chinatown or Little Italy. Moreover, the single commercial street in Manhattan that caters to Brazilian tourists and immigrants and which they call "Little Brazil" is virtually unknown to other residents of the city.

Much of the city's sizeable Brazilian population actually lives in Queens, more specifically in Astoria and neighboring Long Island City, traditional working class neighborhoods with large Greek, Italian and Hispanic populations. In fact, 60 percent of the Brazilian immigrants I studied lived in Queens, with the majority in Astoria.[1] Aside from Brazilians, Astoria is also home to other recent arrivals: Filipinos, Bangladeshis, Indians, Chinese and Irish. It is an attractive locale to Brazilians and other immigrants new to the city because of its proximity to Manhattan, where most have jobs, and its relatively inexpensive rents.

Astoria is a neighborhood of low-rise apartment buildings, modest attached two-family houses and the dominating presence of an elevated subway line that shrouds its main commercial thoroughfare in constant gloom. But despite its ethnic diversity, there are occasional clues to the Brazilian presence there—the odd Brazilian flag poking out of an apartment window, the cramped shops stocked with Brazilian food products, newspapers, magazines and videos, and the travel agencies featuring inexpensive flights to Rio do Janeiro and São Paulo. Aside from Manhattan's Little Brazil, Astoria is the only place in New York City that has a cluster of Brazilian-owned businesses—grocery stores, remittance and travel agencies, call car companies, a unisex beauty salon, and several bars and eating places—catering to the needs of the immigrant community.

---

1. Brazilians are not limited to Queens; about 30 percent live in Manhattan with smaller concentrations in the city's other boroughs.

Little Brazil Street, West 46th Street in midtown Manhattan, has shops, restaurants and other businesses catering to Brazilian immigrants and tourists alike.

NUMBERS, NUMBERS, NUMBERS

The most questionable feature of Brazilian immigration to the United States is its size. It is impossible to gauge with any degree of certainty how many Brazilians live in New York City or other cities in the United States or in the country as a whole. The problem can be illustrated with just a few figures. The 1990 census recorded only 9,200 Brazilians in the New York City (4,400 in Queens, 2,900 in Manhattan and 1,000 in Brooklyn), while the local Brazilian consulate estimates that 80,000 to 100,000 Brazilians live in the greater New York metropolitan area. The Brazilian foreign office puts the number at 230,000! Or take the widely differing estimates for Massachusetts. According to the 1990 U.S. Census, Massachusetts is home to 10,461 Brazilians, a mere 1.6 percent of the state's foreign-born population. But the Brazilian government estimates that there are 150,000 Brazilians living in the Boston metropolitan area alone, while a study done for the Catholic Archdiocese of Boston came up with a figure of 150,000 Brazilians statewide (Klintowitz 1996).

And the situation is no clearer at the national level. While the 1990 census found only 94,000 Brazilians living in the United States, other estimates are up to six times that magnitude. For example, the Brazilian government estimates that 500,000 Brazilians live in the United States, while *Veja*, a Brazilian newsweekly similar to *Time*, puts the figure at over 600,000. Clearly, the actual number lies somewhere between these absurdly divergent figures, probably in the neighborhood of 350,000 to 400,000 Brazilians for the country as a whole.

These contradictions are summarized by comparing the figures in Tables 1.1 and 1.2.

TABLE 1.1   1990 UNITED STATES CENSUS FOREIGN-BORN BRAZILIANS

State	Numbers
California	14,797
New York	14,403
Florida	10,461
Massachusetts	10,186
New Jersey	10,133
All other states	34,043
Foreign-Born Brazilians in the U.S.:	94,023

Source: United States Department of Commerce, 1990

TABLE 1.2   BRAZILIAN POPULATION IN THE U.S. METROPOLITAN AREAS WITH MAJOR CONCENTRATIONS

City	Numbers
New York	230,000
Boston	150,000
Miami	130,000
Washington, DC	47,000
Houston	15,000
San Francisco	15,000
Los Angeles	13,000
Total:	600,000

Source: Brazilian Ministry of External Affairs, 1996

Why Are They Invisible?

Why are these figures so divergent? Why are estimates for the number of Brazilians living in the United States as much as five times greater than the number recorded in official census statistics? The major cause of these absurdly inconsistent figures is that a significant but unknown percentage of Brazilians living in the United States are undocumented immigrants. In New York City, for example, just over half of the Brazilians I studied were undocumented and estimates suggest that perhaps one-third of Brazilian immigrants in this country lack papers (De Souza 1996). They arrive in the United States on tourist visas, take jobs, overstay their visas and thereby become undocumented. Immigrants who are in the United States illegally—no matter what their nationality—try to maintain a low profile and, in doing so, are very difficult to count.

Aside from the issue of legal status, I also found that most Brazilians simply were not interested in participating in the U.S. census. As we will see in the pages to follow, most Brazilians view their stay in the United States as temporary. They think of themselves as sojourners in this country rather than as true immigrants; given the transitory nature of their residence, they see nothing to gain and possibly something to lose by making their presence known by filling out official census forms (Margolis 1995a).

Yet another reason why Brazilians have been consistently undercounted in the U.S. census and other studies that classify and tally immigrants is their fuzzy race or ethnicity. The classification of Brazilians is problematic because they do not easily fit into any standard American ethnic or racial category. They cannot be classified as "Hispanic"—a category used in the census and in other statistical surveys—because they speak Portuguese, not Spanish. And while they are "Latin Americans," this is a geographical, not an ethnic designation. Then, too, using racial instead of ethnic terms also leaves the issue unresolved because the Brazilian population is neither black nor white; Brazilians may be either "race" or any shade in between (Margolis 1989).

Here is an example of how some of these issues come into play in assigning ethnic identity: A Professor of Portuguese at Brown University was asked to talk to Portuguese-speaking children at several public schools in the Boston area. He assumed that they were the children of immigrants from Portugal since there has long been a Portuguese community in the region. But as soon as he arrived at the first school and heard the children's accents, he immediately realized that 90 or 95 percent of the children were Brazilian, *not* Portuguese. The same ratio held for the other classrooms he visited at different grade levels. The bilingual education teachers were aware that the children in their classes were from Brazil not Portugal, but the schools never informed state authorities who fund the classes because most of the Brazilians are children of undocumented immigrants; by simply referring to them as "Portuguese-speakers" their legal status did not become an issue.

As a result of these factors, Brazilians are invisible even when compared to other undocumented immigrant groups in the United States. For example, in a study of undocumented immigrants, Brazil is not even listed among the top fifty countries worldwide in the number of its citizens living illegally in the United States (Warren 1995). Since countries with as few as 6,000 undocumented aliens are included in the list, the assumption is that there are fewer than 6,000 Brazilians with undocumented status living in this country, an absurd figure that bears no relation to reality.

WHY DO THEY COME?

While there are doubts as to the actual number of Brazilian immigrants living in the United States, there is little question about what motivates them to leave Brazil and seek their fortune abroad. Brazilians in the United States often describe themselves as "economic refugees" or "economic prospectors" and these images are born out in my own study. Nearly two-thirds of the immigrants I interviewed in New York City cited economic or professional reasons for coming to this country. There are two sides to the equation that explain the economic motivations of Brazilian immigrants: on the one side are the factors that prodded them to leave Brazil in the first place, and on the other are the conditions that led them to emigrate to the United States.

Brazil has been beset by endemic economic problems for at least two decades—low wages, underemployment, a high cost of living, economic insecurity, and until 1994, hyperinflation. The chaotic economic situation in Brazil is evident from a few statistics: since 1980 Brazil has had four currencies, five wage and price freezes, nine economic stabilization programs, and an inflation index of 146 *billion percent* (Brooke 1993)! But it is not these lifeless statistics that cause Brazilians to leave their homeland, but the real life conditions that arise from them.

During the first decade of significant emigration from Brazil—roughly 1984 to 1994—a major culprit in the exodus was the nation's out-of-control inflation. Always high, inflation soared during the late 1980s and early 1990s, reaching over 2,500 percent annually by 1994, a rate of 40 percent a month. To make some sense of these figures, consider the following: if the Brazilian currency had not been adjusted to keep up with inflation, a *cafezinho* (a Brazilian-style expresso) that cost 15 *cruzeiros* in 1980 would have sold for 22 billion *cruzeiros* by mid-1993 (Brooke 1993; 1994a; 1994b).[2]

In 1994 the Brazilian government instituted an economic plan that brought down the rate of inflation. But then prices for goods and services skyrocketed and within a year the Brazilian media was awash with stories about how middle-class Brazilians were suffering under the new economic program; one headline read "The Middle Class Passes from Euphoria to Bankruptcy." While general inflation was up 35 percent annually—low by Brazilian standards—for the Brazilian middle class it had actually risen by 56 percent. Higher prices for services used primarily by the middle class were to blame. Rent was up over 200 percent; domestic service, 150 percent; barbers and beauty salons, between 90 and 100 percent; restaurant meals, 66 percent; medical care, 60 percent; and school fees, nearly 50 percent. Then, too, goods bought by average middle-class Brazilians also rose and became far more expensive than they are in the United States: a can of Coke cost about 50 percent more in Rio de Janeiro than in Washington DC; a Big Mac, 140 percent more; Levi jeans, 300 percent more; a Sony CD player, 350 percent more, and Reebok sneakers cost almost

---

2. The *cruzeiro* was the Brazilian unit of currency until July 1994 when it was replaced by the *real*. One *real* was worth close to United States $1.00 in late 1996.

four times what they do in the United States (*Veja* 1995a; Araujo 1995; Peluso and Goldberg 1995; Araujo 1995; Cristina 1995).

These price differentials were further aggravated by the fact that Brazilian salaries are much lower than American salaries. In 1995 the average monthly salary in the six largest cities in Brazil was only R$450 or about US$500. Moreover, the price rises occurred without any concurrent increase in middle class income, making it far harder to make ends meet. In order to deal with the crisis, many members of the Brazilian middle class began paying for basic expenses with credit cards. But with high interest rates, bounced checks and unpaid credit cards, bills reached unprecedented numbers and personal bankruptcies soared (Peluso and Goldberg 1995). Thus, despite the relatively low rate of inflation, the Brazilian middle class is still in an economic vise so that many Brazilians continue to see emigration as an option. As one immigrant-in-the-making put it: "Yes, the price of food in the supermarket is the same from one day to the next. But who can afford it? We earn so little!"

Aside from high prices and low wages, another powerful spur to emigration is the inability of some Brazilian immigrants to get jobs in the areas in which they were trained. During my New York study I encountered psychologists, economists, lawyers, teachers, social workers and agronomists who simply could not find full-time jobs that paid reasonable salaries in their own fields. While far more Brazilians than ever before are attending universities and receiving degrees, the number of jobs that call for higher education has not kept pace. The nation's economic difficulties in the 1980s and early 1990s meant that fewer jobs requiring university-level training were created. Thus, many Brazilians with college degrees could only get positions with lower status and lower pay than their educational credentials warranted.

Other would-be immigrants are the Brazilians who had held reasonably good jobs but lost them during the economic downturn. This predicament is depicted in the 1994 *telenovela*, "Our Homeland." A divorced middle-class woman living with her teenage daughter in Rio de Janeiro finds herself unemployed after the magazine where she had worked for fifteen years as chief researcher suddenly folds. What follows is an agonizing discussion between the woman and her daughter about the difficulty of finding a comparable job and the possibility of emigrating to the United States. The daughter is in favor of going, noting caustically that, owing to the nation's dire economic situation, "Brazil doesn't have a middle class anymore."

It is not only soap opera characters that have proclaimed the "death" of the Brazilian middle class. Brazilians in New York City told me that it was now "impossible" to maintain a middle class lifestyle in Brazil. The maelstrom of paltry wages, high prices, few good job opportunities and continued economic uncertainty cast a pall over the lives of untold numbers of middle-class Brazilians. When they look at the future and see little hope of improving their economic situation, emigration, in effect, becomes a "what have I got to lose" option. Moreover, since most immigrants are young and single and do not need much capital to emigrate abroad—the trip is usually financed through personal savings or with loans from family or friends— emigration can be seen as a temporary, low cost personal investment opportunity (Martes 1995a).

What are the factors that make emigration to the United States so attractive? Immigrants are very precise on this point: in striking contrast to jobs in Brazil, jobs in the United States pay high enough wages to permit savings. The figure most often cited is four to one, that is, immigrants can make in one week in the United States what it took four weeks to earn in Brazil. The most basic enticement of emigration is the ability to earn much more money in much less time; what one immigrant called "the economy of time." Brazilians complain that even after working twenty years in Brazil buying a house or even a car is still out of reach of most people. In the United States the wages saved from only one or two year's labor can translate into a down payment on an apartment in Brazil or a nest egg to begin a small business there.

Given a monthly minimum wage of $113 in Brazil (in May 1996) and a per capita gross domestic product only 17 percent of that of the United States, it is little wonder why Brazilians find U.S. wages so appealing (Osava 1996; Schemo 1996).[3] However, it is important to emphasize that we are not dealing with minimum wage workers here. As we will see in the chapter to follow, Brazil-

---

3. In Minas Gerais, a major exporter of immigrants to the U.S., annual per capita income in 1996 was $1,700 (Moura and Cristina 1996).

ian immigrants in New York City are generally middle class and well educated. Before coming to this country most held professional or semi-professional positions that paid good salaries by Brazilian standards. Still, in comparison to what they earn even in the most menial jobs in the United States, Brazilian salaries look feeble indeed.

Many Brazilian immigrants who come to this country are target earners, immigrants who are working to save money to pay for some specific item back home—land, an apartment, a car, a new business. A group of immigrants from the tiny town of Tiros in the Brazilian state of Minas Gerais are an example of target earners who have come up with a novel means to insure that the money they earn at their jobs in New Jersey arrives quickly and safely in their hometown in Brazil. Twice a year they pay the round-trip airfare from New York to Brazil of another immigrant from the town who hand delivers their savings to waiting relatives. The cost of the airline ticket divided among the group of friends is much less than the 10 percent commission that remittance agencies typically charge for wiring money to Brazil. The individual who carries the small fortune in collective savings back to Brazil was chosen as the courier not only because he is a trusted friend, but because he alone among them has a green card. The green card allows him to come and go from the United States as he pleases. The other members of the group are undocumented immigrants and cannot risk the trip to Brazil themselves because they might find it difficult or impossible to return to this country.

Economic motives for coming to the United States often coalesce with other motives. For many Brazilians, emigrating to New York has an added subtext: the experience of living in one of the world's great cities in a country that is so embedded in the Brazilian imagination. The sheer adventure and unending possibilities of the journey are also potent allures. Middle class, urban Brazilians—the background of most immigrants in New York City—are predisposed to the lifestyles of the developed world, most particularly the United States. The appetite for "things international" helps obfuscate the harsh reality of the economic crisis at home, the daily reminder that Brazil is still a third-world nation. Coming to the United States and earning first-world wages—even if they are at the bottom of the local pay scale—provides middle-class Brazilians easy access to the objects that symbolize "first-world modernity" (O'Dougherty 1995:20–21).

Brazil is a land suffused with American images. By saturating the Brazilian public with representations of the good life, American-style, the Brazilian media play an inadvertent role in the emigration flow. Brazilian television and magazines transmit an unending stream of idealized messages about American patterns of consumption and behavior, about American films, American music and American fashions, often obliquely suggesting their hegemony over the homegrown variety. It is not surprising that the opportunity to visit the source of these fanciful images is a powerful draw to aspiring immigrants.

BECOMING AN IMMIGRANT

Once Brazilians decide to emigrate to the United States, the initial step is figuring out how to pay for the trip itself along with the expenses of the early weeks in this country. The next step is getting a U.S. tourist visa. At first glance, financing the move looks like it could be a problem and securing a visa seems like it would be easy. But this is not necessarily the case. In fact, for most Brazilian immigrants in New York City paying for the trip was not a major obstacle. The minimum amount needed for the move to the United States is around $2,000—about $1000 for airfare and $1000 for initial living expenses—although most immigrants bring additional funds in case they have trouble finding work or encounter other unanticipated expenses. About two-thirds of the Brazilians in my New York study paid for the trip from their savings or by selling a car or other personal property or they received financial help from their families in the form of gifts or loans. The remaining third financed the trip through loans, typically installment loans from travel agencies for plane tickets. But there is still another option; an unknown but significant number of Brazilians who are not quite tourists and not quite immigrants. They come to the United States with just enough money to live on for two or three weeks and resolve that if they cannot find work in that time, they will simply hop on a plane and return to Brazil, chalking up the experience as an adventure, an opportunity to see a foreign country.

If financing the trip abroad is relatively easy for most Brazilian immigrants, getting a U.S. tourist visa can be a daunting experience. To be approved for a tourist visa by American consular officers in Brazil, would-be travelers have to show that they have sufficient funds to cover their stay in the United States. More important, they must demonstrate that they have compelling reasons to return to Brazil: a good job or significant property or close family ties there. In other words, they have to prove beyond a reasonable doubt that they have *no* intention of staying in the United States and seeking work, that they are not illegal immigrants-in-the-making.

This is more easily said than done. During the course of my field research, I met individuals in New York City who had been turned down three, four, even five times before getting a tourist visa. New York's Brazilian community is rife with tales about the pursuit of this illusive document, and it is not just Brazilians who want to emigrate to the United States who have problems, but legitimate tourists as well. Moreover, because of the tremendous demand for visas from immigrants and tourists alike, the process of getting one can consume many hours or even days if the aspiring traveler lives far from an American consular office in a major city like Rio de Janeiro or São Paulo.[4]

The long wait for a visa and the bureaucracy involved in applying for one has spawned a host of entrepreneurs who sell everything from spaces on the long snaking line in front of the American Consulate, to visa application forms and *cafezinhos*, tiny cups of strong Brazilian coffee. On a chilly winter morning at 6:45 AM a crowd of well over five hundred people were already standing on line in front of the modern glass building that houses the American consular offices in Rio de Janeiro. One visa seeker was offered 150th place on line for $30. Promptly at 8 AM the American Consulate opens its doors and the human line begins to inch forward. By 10 AM that day's quota of about 500 visa applicants has been

---

4. In 1994, over one-half million U.S. tourist visas were issued to Brazilians and Brazil was the sixth country worldwide in the number of U.S. tourist visas issued to its citizens (U.S. Immigration and Naturalization Service 1996). The vast majority of the visas go to legitimate tourists, not immigrants.

filled and the Consulate shuts its doors. A consular employee informs the people still on line—about 200 on a typical day—that they will have to come back at another time. After spending seven hours over two days on line, a journalist doing a magazine story on the great visa chase finally succeeded in setting foot on American territory at 9:50 AM—ten minutes before closing on the second day. He writes with evident disgust that "visa applicants are made to stand for hours like mendicants in a soup line" (Mac Margolis 1994:48).

Entry into an American Consulate does not guarantee success in obtaining a visa. Visas are not given lightly to aspiring tourists who fit the "immigrant profile," applicants who are young, single and without a steady job. Such applicants, claim American consular officials, have little binding them to Brazil. As such, they are more likely to stay on in the United States after their visa expires to seek work and to wind up as undocumented immigrants. To get a tourist visa an applicant must show a round-trip plane ticket, proof of income and residence and an income tax declaration form. In case of doubt, applicants are interviewed. Interviewers in glass booths ask questions of visa applicants via microphone. "Where are you going? With whom? Why are you going now?" The journalist, pretending he was a tourist in search of a visa, was asked, "Have you ever participated in genocide? Do you intend to enter the United States in order to become involved in subversive or terrorist activities?" Both questions and answers are necessarily broadcast to one and all on line. And word is out that some interviewers give applicants a hard time. "Avoid the woman with the short dark hair, if you can," was the advice of Brazilians who had been through the gruelling application process. After the interview, visa seekers are told to return in the afternoon to learn their fate.

Legendary tales of visa denials quickly spread among hopeful travelers, be they immigrants or legitimate tourists. Around the time of the 1994 World Cup, for example, it was said that the American Consulate in São Paulo was refusing to issue tourist visas to Brazilians planning to attend the games in the United States, the assumption being that many would stay on and seek work. Tales of individual frustration are legion. One woman, a nurse, applied for a tourist visa four times over three years and was turned down each time. Lacking significant property in Brazil or a high enough income, she was judged a likely visa over-stayer by consular personnel. Then there is the case of the mother of a Brazilian journalist who has lived in New York for years. She planned to visit her son, his American wife and granddaughter but was denied a visa. Despite substantial personal assets, be-cause she is retired and has a close relative living in the United States, she too was deemed a potential immigrant.

Some enterprising immigrants make up elaborate job histories or borrow money to inflate their bank balances to prove to consu-lar personnel that they are financially well off in Brazil and have no intention of staying in the United States to look for work. Such subterfuge is especially common among Brazilians from Minas Gerais who have infamous reputations as visa overstayers among American consular employees. Some *mineiros*—as natives of the state are called—buy fake birth certificates to "prove" that they come from another part of Brazil believing that this will enhance their chances of getting a visa. Brazilians who are turned down for visas in their own names occasionally travel on someone else's passport with the coveted U.S. tourist visa already stamped in it.

The difficulty many Brazilians encounter getting tourist visas to the United States and the boorish treatment that a few receive when they arrive in this country has made headlines in Brazil. In-deed, the indignity suffered by some Brazilians upon entry into the United States has resulted in at least two lawsuits against the U.S. government. An article in the well respected newsmagazine, *The Economist*, reports the unhappy experience of some Brazilian travelers. One man from São Paulo—a real estate agent of consid-erable means who had come to this country to see his compatriots play in the World Cup—was accused of carrying a false passport when he arrived at New York's Kennedy Airport and was imme-diately seized by U.S. immigration officials. He was held for fif-teen hours, interrogated and denied contact with his family, lawyers or consular personnel until he "voluntarily" signed a de-portation order and was put on the next plane to Brazil.

Despite forceful efforts to deny tourist visas to individuals suspected of having immigrant intentions, what most Americans do not realize is that it is actually quite easy to be transformed into an "illegal" after arriving in this country. Once getting passed immigration inspection at Kennedy Airport or any other U.S. port of entry, the traveler is essentially home free because no system exists for keeping track of any foreign visitor, whether legitimate tourist or would-be immigrant.

ON TO A NEW LAND

After their return to Brazil, Pedro and Esther—the couple in the Brazilian soap opera "My Homeland"—recount the story of their arrival in the United States to relatives in Rio de Janeiro. The couple took a charter flight to Orlando, Florida under the pretense of visiting Disney World with their three year old son. When they went through customs Esther was nervous because of the four gargantuan suitcases that accompanied them. "What's in those?" asked the customs agent. "Just clothes and toys to play for my son," answered Esther in her uncertain English, knowing full well that their entry to the United States would be stymied if the agent actually inspected the contents of their luggage. There he would have found Esther's one year supply of birth control pills, recipes for Brazilian dishes, small household effects and all manner of other items that would *not* be what the average foreign tourist packed for a two-week Florida vacation. But the suitcases were not opened, the family's tourist visas passed muster, and after a week's stay with friends in Miami, the couple headed for New York City to look for jobs.

Pedro and Esther's story is a common one because after New York, Florida is the most popular arrival point for Brazilian emigrating to the United States. It is also the route favored by families with children since Disney World is the destination of tens of thousands of legitimate Brazilian tourists who arrive in the Sunshine State annually.

But whether one arrives in Florida, New York or Los Angeles, the primary ports of entry for Brazilian immigrants to the United States, the passage through immigration and customs is a nerve wracking experience. Even though most immigrants-to-be come to the United States with valid passports and tourist visas, this does not assure automatic entrée into this country. If immigration officers suspect that an arriving passenger is not a legitimate tourist, the person is detained for questioning.

Why are some travelers suspected of being immigrants? There are several clues that a visitor actually intends to stay in this country and seek work; an inordinate amount of luggage for a short vacation stay or clothes that are inappropriate to the tourist's destination—a heavy winter coat packed for a trip to Miami, for example. Other signs of permanence are items that hint of a long-term sojourn such as Esther's one year supply of birth control pills or several months worth of prescription medications.

Having a close relative in this country also may alert immigration authorities. The reasoning is that kin can provide a haven to newcomers, housing them and helping them find work. This is why immigrants-in-the-making are warned by their experienced compatriots to deny, if asked, that they have family ties or even know anyone living in the United States. Finally, visitors who arrive with too little money to pay for a New York or Florida "vacation" are targeted for further questioning since this may indicate that the traveler has come not for a short-term trip but for a long-term job. As such, most Brazilians carry at least $1,000 with them—the minimum amount thought necessary to escape suspicion—even if they have to borrow the money from relatives or friends.

While most Brazilian immigrants fly to New York, Miami or Los Angeles, a few arrive in the United States via the route most often associated with undocumented aliens; they take the long, perilous and costly journey from Brazil to the United States through Mexico. Although I met very few Brazilian immigrants in New York City who had entered the United States via Mexico, Brazilian immigrants living in Boston and Newark are somewhat more likely to take this route.

The Mexican connection is the path of last resort for Brazilian immigrants traveling to the United States. The trip through Mexico is not only more arduous and riskier, it costs three to five times as much as the more direct air route from Rio de Janeiro or São Paulo to New York or Florida. A package that includes airfare from Brazil to Mexico, transportation to the U.S. border, the assistance of a *coyote* for the actual crossing, travel to a U.S. border city and a one-way plane ticket to the final destination can cost upwards of $5000. Contrast this with the $1000 to $2000 round-trip airfare on a direct flight from Brazil to the United States paid by travelers who enter legally as tourists.

The serious drawbacks—monetary and otherwise—of coming to the United States by way of Mexico are such that only Brazilian immigrants who cannot gain entry to this country any other way even consider this route. These are individuals who have been turned down again and again for tourist visas because American consular personnel in Brazil suspect them of having immigrant tendencies. They may be denied visas because they come from Minas Gerais, the Brazilian state notorious for exporting immigrants, or because they cannot demonstrate that they have adequate financial resources to make a return to Brazil likely. In either case, it is ironic that it is usually the less well-off who have to take the more costly and difficult Mexican route to achieve their goal of emigrating to this country.

Brazilian immigrants aside, the Mexican route is not as important as it once was. Contrary to popular stereotypes of undocumented immigrants as clandestine border crossers, today less than half of the illegal immigrants in this country actually enter the United States on foot by way of the Mexican border. Nearly all of the rest—about six of every ten undocumented immigrants—jet into one of the nation's major international airports. They enter legally as tourists, students or temporary employees and only become illegal when they stay on in the United States after their visas have expired (Fix and Passel 1994).

Then, too, when Americans think of an illegal border crosser, what immediately comes to mind is a young male from rural Mexico. This was, indeed, an accurate portrait because, until recently, OTMs—other than Mexicans—the term used for non-Mexicans by the U.S. Immigration Service—accounted for a very tiny percentage of individuals who crossed the border illegally. But this is changing, and in the early 1990s the number of OTMs apprehended by the Border Patrol began inching upward. Apprehensions also have become much more international. Not only are OTMs now from neighboring Guatemala and El Salvador, but the Border Patrol increasingly reports the arrest of Serbians, Koreans, Turks, Indians, Chinese, Brazilians and Poles.

First Things First

After arriving in the United States, Brazilians, like other immigrants, have two immediate priorities: first, finding a place to live, then finding a job. For many, the key to both is having relatives and friends in this country. Over two-thirds of the Brazilians in my New York study stayed with friends or relatives during their first days or weeks in the city or received help from them finding work. Typically, a job would be arranged for a new immigrant at a brother's or sister's or cousin's place of employment or through a friend's prior contacts in the city. These immigrant networks meant that some new arrivals were able to start work almost immediately.

New immigrants need something more than just connections to get a job. They also need a social security card. Here, too, immigrant networks and immigrant knowledge come into play. There is a thriving document "industry" in New York, Los Angeles and other cities with large immigrant populations. Since immigration reform legislation passed the U.S. Congress in 1986, employers are required to ask for work papers before offering a job. But many employers will quickly hire a person once some kind of "legal" document is shown, including a social security card. The law does not require employers to authenticate any one of the myriad documents that the new hire may show to "prove" work eligibility. As such, all one needs is a counterfeit social security card—a "*social*" as Brazilians call it—the life blood of immigrant employment. A *social* is usually purchased early in the immigrant's sojourn in this country for about $150.

Not all Brazilian immigrants could count on the assistance of relatives or friends to help them find a job; about one-quarter of those I interviewed traveled to the United States alone and knew no one when they arrived. They carried with them little more than the name and address of an inexpensive hotel or the phone number of a rooming house that caters to Brazilian immigrants. Some of these lone voyagers looked back on their first weeks in the city with a sense of wonder and pride that they had been able to endure the ordeal. They told tales of sleeping in train stations or in shoddy hotels in Times Square, of wandering city streets amid the alien cacophony of a language they did not understand, and of feeling disconnected from the teeming metropolis around them.

Whether they arrive in New York alone or accompanied by family or friends, most Brazilian immigrants find permanent quarters within a few weeks. These they share with other Brazilians, sometimes compatriots they met after coming to the city.

Few Brazilians live alone; in fact, only ten percent of those I studied in New York did so. The reasons are two-fold: cost and custom. New York is an expensive city and no single item costs more than rent. As such, having friends and relatives share housing and utility bills is critical given the aim of most Brazilians—at least when they first arrive in this country—of saving as much money as quickly as possible for the return to Brazil.

Cost is not the only issue. Living alone in order to have one's private "space" is an arrangement that strikes Brazilians as rather odd. Even if they could afford to live alone, most Brazilians would choose to live with friends or relatives because in the Brazilian scheme of things living alone means being lonely. In fact, Americans and Brazilians have a very different sense of and need for privacy. Let me illustrate with a personal anecdote. When I first went to Brazil to do summer field work I was a twenty-two year old graduate student. While there I lived with the family of the administrator of a sugar estate, the site of my field research. Even though the administrator's house was large and had rooms to spare, I was told that I would be sharing the small bedroom of his 12-year old daughter so that she could keep me company and I would not feel "too lonely" being so far from home, parents and other relatives. Needless to say, my North American sense of privacy was none too pleased with this arrangement!

So both money and cultural notions of conviviality enter into the residential choices of Brazilian immigrants in New York City. This is why a married couple will take in one or two paying boarders and why a number of friends will rent a small apartment together and put up with the crowded conditions that inevitably result. Brazilians even have a word for such places. They call them *puleiros,* Portuguese slang for "chicken coops." Whether in an apartment or a rooming house that caters to new immigrants, a *puleiro* is a place that houses a lot of people in very cramped quarters.

Living in a *puleiro* is typically a passing phase in the life cycle of recent arrivals from Brazil. Researchers call such living arrangements "no family households" made up of single people sharing an apartment or domestic servants who live in the homes of their employers (Chavez 1989). People who reside in them are usually single migrants who plan to get a job, make money and then return home. These households become less common as immigrants turn into settlers. Given that most Brazilian immigrants are new to this country and that most view themselves as temporary sojourners, it is not surprising that nearly 40 percent of Brazilians in my study lived in households of this type. Most of the rest live in households comprised of kin. New York Brazilians are about evenly divided between those who live in simple family households that consist of a married couple with or without children or a single parent family and those who reside in complex family households made up of varying combinations of relatives. The importance of multiple family incomes can be gauged from the fact that three-quarters of these households had two or more family wage-earners.

Since the driving ambition of Brazilian immigrants, at least initially, is to save money as quickly as possible for the return home, many are reluctant to spend their hard earned dollars setting up their New York residences. After all, why put money into living accommodations when they are only temporary? Still, certain basic items are required and some Brazilians furnish their living quarters with American castoffs. Abandoned mattresses, couches, chairs, tables, electrical appliances, even clothes, are sometimes retrieved from garbage cans and trash pickups. Brazilians refer to this as their "garbage decor." The living patterns I observed among Brazilian immigrants in New York City are similar to those of other new immigrants. Immigrants of whatever nationality are often willing to live in crowded, austere settings under conditions that would never be tolerated at home. However unpleasant their current living arrangements, they are transient and worth the inconvenience, many immigrants conclude. After all, they are saving for their future and perhaps, for the future of their children.

THE GREAT OUTCRY

Before we continue with our portrait of Brazilians as a recent wave in the sea of transnational migrants to the United States, one issue that is central to contemporary American discourse on immigration must be raised. This is the outcry in our country against immigrants in general, and "illegal aliens" in particular. Why do politicians and pundits denounce the immigrant "invasion" which, they claim, drains our nation of its limited social and economic resources?

The answer lies in what I call immigrant blame, the practice of holding immigrants responsible for trends in the nation's economy that have little or nothing to do with them. To be sure, this is not a new phenomenon in our history. At least since the 1880s, immigrants have been accused of taking jobs away from native workers and lowering their wages. They have been charged with contributing to poverty and with wresting social services from more deserving citizens. The only thing that has changed are the nationalities of the immigrants said to be responsible for these social ills (Espenshade 1995).

The immigrant blame of today can only be understood against the backdrop of changes in the American economy that have occurred over the last two decades, changes that have adversely affected a broad swath of the American middle class. Immigrants as targets of blame serve as surrogates for the sense of insecurity and unease that have become a badge of contemporary American economic life. In essence, the growing inequalities in wealth and income and widespread wage deterioration have been diverted onto the backs of immigrants.

The inequality in earnings between the top 20 percent and the bottom 20 percent of wage earners in this country has doubled over the last 25 years as wages for most Americans entered a slow decline. By the early 1970s the median wage of American men working full-time had begun its descent; since then men's earnings have fallen by more than 10 percent (Thurow 1995). And, while the pain of lower wages was once limited to non-college educated, blue collar men, the decline has now spread to higher-wage, white collar men (Mishel and Bernstein 1996).

For a number of years the decrease in average male wages was not reflected in a decline in household income because women made up the slack by taking jobs in record numbers (Margolis 1984). Household income, in fact, rose slowly until 1989. But in that year median real wages for women working full-time also began to fall. As a result, after correcting for inflation, median family income fell seven percent from 1989 to 1993—the first such four-year stretch since World War II—and by 1994, the bottom 95 percent of families in this country had incomes below their 1989 level (Thurow 1995; Mishel and Bernstein 1996).

Jobs also have become less secure over the last several years, intensifying the economic uncertainty of many Americans. Moreover, the consequences of losing a job today are more troubling than in the past. As the net worth of middle income families declined in the early 1990s, they had fewer resources to fall back on in case of job loss (Mishel and Bernstein 1996). Then, too, fewer jobs now provide the health insurance and pension benefits that most middle-class Americans have come to expect.

The reasons for these changes are complicated and involve deregulation, the weakened bargaining power of employees, the shift to service sector employment and the globalization of the economy. But the truth is that immigrants probably have done less to depress the wages of low-skilled American workers than the millions of American women who have entered the labor force over the last three decades. The growing inequality of household income also has a demographic cause. As more single working mothers populate the lower end of the income scale, more upper end households have two well-paid professional wage earners, making for a greater income spread (Wright 1995). And so, while new arrivals in this country logically have little or nothing to do with these complex changes, holding immigrants accountable for them has a simple and direct appeal. And it clearly makes for better politics to blame "aliens" for these painful economic shifts than to cite vague American "economic and demographic trends" as the culprits.

2

Brazilian Immigrants: A Portrait

If you were to ask an average American to describe an "illegal immigrant," he or she would doubtless say something like: "Oh, a Mexican. Probably a young guy from a poverty stricken village in rural Mexico. Someone who's not well educated—maybe he's been through primary school, that's all. Someone who's real poor, from a very poor family that lives in a shack and maybe doesn't have enough to eat." Although many Brazilian immigrants in the United States are, in fact, undocumented—recall that just over half in my New York study were—they bear absolutely no resemblance to the stereotypical "illegal" of this description. Brazilian immigrants in New York City and, it appears, in other Brazilian communities around the United States are overwhelmingly middle and lower-middle class and many are well educated.

This portrait is based on data gathered on the social class and educational level of immigrants in New York's Brazilian community. Social class is difficult to measure and in my own study I employed two means to define it. First, I looked at objective criteria to judge class affiliation—occupation and property ownership of immigrants and their parents in Brazil and years of schooling. Then I sought self-identification; I asked Brazilian immigrants to what social class they belonged. Finally, based on all of this information, I recorded my own observations of social class membership (Table 2.1 combines and summarizes these findings).

TABLE 2.1   BRAZIL'S SOCIAL CLASSES

Social Class	Percentage of Brazil's Population
Upper & Upper-middle Class	6 percent
Middle & Lower-middle Class	34 percent
Working Class	34 percent
Abject Poverty	26 percent

Source: adapted from Kottak, 1990

How do the data on social class in the immigrant community compare to that in Brazil as a whole? Clearly, Brazilian immigrants in New York City represent only a portion of Brazil's social hierarchy. One index of social class—buying power—has been used in Table 2.1 as an indirect gauge of the nation's class structure. A word of explanation: the scale is based on the disposable income of Brazilians, the amount and proportion of household income that remains after basic living expenses are met for food, housing, clothing, utilities, and so on. The greater the amount and percentage of income left over after these expenses are paid, the more disposable income a household is said to have, the higher its social class.

Now compare the distribution of social classes in the national scale above to Table 2.2, my own data on the social class of Brazilian immigrants in New York City. In the national scale the four top classes (upper through lower-middle) make-up 40 percent of the Brazilian population, while about 90 percent of Brazilian immigrants in New York City fall into one of these top strata. We see nearly the reverse of these proportions when we look at the bottom rungs of the social ladder. While the two poorest classes (working and abject poverty) account for 60 percent of the Brazilian population, only 10 percent of the immigrant population in New York is so classified. In sum, Brazilian immigrants in the city are decidedly more middle class than their compatriots back home.

Social class must be contextualized, that is, viewed from the perspective of the "sending" society. What does it mean to be middle class in Brazil? The Brazilian middle class is sometimes defined as those with "um collarinho e gravata"—a collar and tie—because a major marker of middle-class membership there is white collar employment. In Brazil, people who work with their

Table 2.2 Social Class of Brazilian Immigrants in New York City

Social Class	Percentage of Population
Upper-middle Class	11 percent
Middle & Lower-middle Class	79 percent
Lower Class	10 percent

hands, people who do manual labor, are, by definition, not middle class. This is probably why middle class Brazilian families are far more likely than their American counterparts to employ domestic servants in their homes. It would be unthinkable for a middle-class Brazilian housewife to scrub floors or wash clothes.

Almost no Brazilian immigrants in New York City were employed in occupations requiring manual labor when they lived in Brazil; nor for that matter, were their parents. Close to one-quarter of the parents of immigrants in my study were business owners, which is strong evidence of membership in the middle or lower-middle class in Brazilian society. The large proportion of professionals in this immigrant community—also nearly one-quarter of those in my New York study—is another clear indicator of middle class status. Professionals represented in this immigrant population included journalists, engineers, agronomists, lawyers, social workers and psychologists—all occupations associated with the middle strata of Brazilian society.

Not all of New York's Brazilians held such relatively lofty occupations back home. Lower-middle class Brazilians are also well represented in this immigrant community. Many émigrés were nurses and elementary school teachers, scandalously underpaid professions in Brazil. Others owned small businesses—bars and restaurants, grocery stores, auto repair shops, pharmacies—that were ravaged by their homeland's troubled economy. Interestingly, the social class of the immigrant family in the Brazilian soap opera *Patria Minha* is unlike that of the typical Brazilian immigrant in New York City. Pedro's father is depicted as a busdriver, one of his brothers is an automobile mechanic and the other brother drives a taxi. The family lives in a modest house in a Rio *favela*, one of the city's famed hillside shantytowns. Both the occupations and residence reflect working-class not middle-class roots in Brazil, which is the actual background of the majority of Brazilian immigrants in New York City.

Patterns of property ownership among the city's Brazilian immigrants and their parents is yet another sign of middle-class origins. In Brazil, to own a major item of property like an automobile is to be middle or lower-middle class. As it turned out, over 60 percent of the immigrants in my study owned significant property in Brazil—land, a house or apartment, a car—and an even higher proportion of their parents—84 percent—owned similar property.

Data on the education of New York's Brazilian immigrant community also reflects their relatively elite class status since New York-based Brazilians have an uncommonly high level of schooling. Over three-quarters of the Brazilian immigrants in my study have at least a high school education; nearly half have some university training; and close to one-third have university degrees. To put these figures in perspective consider the fact that in 1990 only 28 percent of the Brazilian population had finished high school and just 12 percent had gone on to a university. The educational level of Brazilian immigrants in New York City is impressive even by U.S. standards; after all, just under one-quarter of all Americans have college degrees.

The social class make-up of New York's Brazilian immigrant community also holds the key to its racial make-up. Here, too, New York's Brazilians are not representative of their nation's population because most cluster at the lighter end of the color spectrum. In my own study, 83 percent of the Brazilians I interviewed were white, 8 percent were light mulatto or mulatto, and 8 percent were black. Thus, blacks and other "people of color," to use the Brazilian phrase, account for only about 16 percent of the city's Brazilian immigrant community, a fraction of the 45 percent reported in the 1990 census for Brazil as a whole (Fundação Instituto Brasileiro de Geografia e Estatística 1994).

What is the relationship between race and class in Brazil? Brazilian racial types are not randomly distributed across the nation's social classes and people of color are over-represented at the lower ranks of Brazilian society, under-represented in the middle sectors, and nearly absent among the nation's tiny elite. Thus, if Brazilian immigration is mostly a middle and lower-middle class phenomenon—as it appears to be in New York City—it is not surprising that the immigrant population is lighter than the nation as a whole.

Self-Images

The dominance of the middle classes in the city's Brazilian immigrant population is further confirmed by the perceptions of the immigrants themselves. Most of those interviewed agreed that the vast majority of their compatriots come from the middle sectors of Brazilian society, with neither Brazil's elite nor her impoverished masses present to any significant degree. Of course, there are wealthy Brazilians in New York, but they come as tourists not as immigrants, or they belong to a small group of executives that run the city's Brazilian banks, airlines and corporations. Similarly, there are very few individuals in New York's immigrant community who would be considered poor by Brazilian standards. After all, Brazil's poor—who have to struggle daily just to meet their most basic needs—are unlikely candidates for international migration.

Still, I discovered a baffling phenomenon while researching social class in New York's Brazilian community. Even though there are very few poor Brazilians in it, many middle class immigrants denied that this was so, insisting that many of their compatriots in the city come from the lower rungs of Brazilian society. They consistently described a portion of immigrant society as poor, uneducated, unsophisticated, and from humble roots. Or, as one Brazilian told me, "Ninety-five percent of the Brazilian immigrants in New York City don't even have a high school education."

What is curious is that I was never able to find such people, although I certainly tried. Whenever someone mentioned this enigmatic group, I always asked: Who are they? Where do they live? How can I get in touch with them? But the answer was always the same: "Well, I don't know any of them personally. I just see Brazilians like that on the street or hear them in the subway speaking ungrammatical Portuguese."

This same illusive band of Brazilians was also said to be divorced from city life and its myriad attractions. "They only come to America to make money." I was told again and again,

"They are basically mercenary. They live in these terribly crowded apartments in awful conditions so they can save money. They have no interest in anything else here. They hardly know New York—they don't learn English—and all they talk about is Brazil. They just stick together and work and work. That's all they do."

Remittances—the money that immigrants send home—provide an important clue to social class, including the purported existence of a sizeable group of poor Brazilians in New York City. In Brazil, as well as in other countries, the families of immigrants that regularly rely on remittance money to meet their living expenses are usually less well-off and from a poorer segment of their own society than the families of immigrants who do not need a routine infusion of foreign cash to pay their bills. As such, remittances can be used as a yardstick of social class affiliation.

Although I found that about half of the immigrants I studied regularly or occasionally sent money home, most who regularly sent remittances were not, in fact, sending money to support their families in Brazil. Instead, they were sending it to build a nest egg for their own return home or to pay off a personal debt incurred for their trip to New York. In other words, I found very few Brazilian immigrants who provided routine financial support for their families in Brazil, further confirmation that members of Brazil's lower class are few and far between in the city's Brazilian immigrant community.

I was told by Brazilian friends that I was unable to locate members of this group because educated Brazilian immigrants were embarrassed to introduce me—a North American academic—to their unschooled compatriots. But, after much probing I eventually came to doubt the existence of a sizable lower stratum in New York's Brazilian population and began to refer to it as "the phantom lower class." What I think explains this phantom lower class is the tendency of Brazilians to point to some vague group of "others" as being poorer, less educated, more mercenary or in some other way inferior to themselves and their own social group. Such common cultural discourse must be particularly reassuring to middle and lower-middle class Brazilian immigrants whose customary social standing has been undermined by the low status jobs they hold in New York City. "We may not be well-off now," they are, in effect, saying, but "at least *we* come from good families and we're well educated—*not like those Brazilians."

NOT THE HUDDLED MASSES

It has long been recognized that it is usually not the very poor who migrate internationally or become undocumented immigrants when they reach their destination. Thus, the class origins and high education levels of New York's Brazilian immigrants are not exceptional. Many other recent immigrants to the United States—Peruvians, Koreans, Argentines, and Indians, to name a few—have middle class roots and their educational credentials are comparable to or even surpass those of the American population as a whole.

Why, in many cases, is it not the "huddled masses" of developing nations but their relatively well-off citizens who seek their fortunes as immigrants abroad? The relatively well-off have what is generally unavailable to the poorer elements in their own societies: the financial resources and the information needed to migrate internationally. In other words, when members of the middle strata are discouraged by economic conditions at home—when they cannot find decent jobs or are fed up with low wages or out of control inflation—they are the ones who have the discretionary income to pay for the high cost of moving abroad and the knowledge and social contacts that enable them to do so. This is particularly true of members of the urban middle class who have more ready access to the services and resources needed by potential immigrants.

Just consider what it usually takes to travel to a geographically distant foreign country, be it for purposes of tourism or emigration. First, one must decide where to go and then find out how to get there—airfares, flight schedules, perhaps bus or train schedules if the trip involves travel to an international airport. Then one must know how to obtain—and be able to pay for—the documents needed for the trip, usually a passport and visa and sometimes immunization records. Knowledge about one's destination is also useful, if not essential—the rate of currency exchange, the expense of travel from foreign airport to destination city, the price and location of lodging and food, the cost of public transportation, and the list could go on. In the case of would-be immigrants, additional information is usually needed: Job opportunities at the destination abroad and the costs of living there, to cite just two obvious examples.

Another factor that clearly gives an advantage to middle class immigrants are the bureaucratic requirements for obtaining travel documents. The comparatively affluent usually have an easier time securing them. Recall that when Brazilians go to the American Consulate in Rio de Janeiro or São Paulo seeking tourist visas, they must demonstrate to the satisfaction of consular personnel that they have sufficient financial resources—a good job or significant property—to tie them to Brazil, making it less likely that they will stay in the United States to seek work and more likely that they will return home. Today in Brazil the obstacles placed in the path of prospective travelers to the United States give middle-class Brazilians a distinct advantage over their poorer compatriots, in effect, making this immigrant flow more middle class than might otherwise be the case.

Then, too, since information about economic opportunities in the destination country is crucial in the decision to migrate, immigrants tend to go to places where they have contacts. After all, information—as well as aid and comfort—is more likely to be available to individuals who already have friends and relatives living in the migration locale. If, therefore, middle-class Brazilians have family or friends who have already emigrated abroad, they are more likely than their poorer compatriots to have access to such information and support. In fact, for some Brazilian families, having a relative in the United States is considered "chic," it is a sign of status. They say they have a relative "living in America," not "working in America" (Martes 1995b).

FOLLOW THE LEADER

There is another intriguing dimension to social class and international migration. Research suggests that international migration is often sequenced by social class, with middle class immigrants paving the way for their homeland's less prosperous citizens (Piore 1979). It is only after information networks that facilitate international migration have been established—travel and remittance agencies, visa brokers, and the like—that would-be immigrants from the lower social strata are able to follow the migratory path abroad blazed by their nation's more affluent citizens.

Similar factors may also explain the geographical distribution of Brazilian immigrants in various cities in the United States. Social class, educational level, place of origin in Brazil, and place of residence in the United States all appear to be connected. In the Boston metropolitan area Brazilians from Governador Valadares, the famed "sending community" mentioned in the last chapter, are more likely to be from lower-middle class or even working class families than are immigrants from other parts of Brazil. Many Valadarenses in the Boston area come from the families of farmers, schoolteachers, small shopkeepers, and military men, while immigrants from Rio de Janeiro and São Paulo are more often the children of professionals—doctors, lawyers and businessmen (Badgley 1994). Similar enclaves of lower-middle class and possibly working class Valadarenses exist in Danbury, Connecticut and Newark, New Jersey. In New York, where the vast majority of Brazilians are middle class, there are relatively few Valadarenses, most immigrants having been "big city kids"—residents of Belo Horizonte, Rio de Janeiro or São Paulo—before emigrating to the United States.

Educational differences among Brazilian immigrants follow along similar lines. In Boston, Brazilian immigrants from Rio de Janeiro and São Paulo—like their counterparts in New York—are apt to have at least some university training, while most of those from Governador Valadares and the surrounding towns have not gone beyond high school. To summarize: Brazilian immigrants from small cities like Governador Valadares are likely to come from more modest backgrounds and have less education than those from the nation's large metropolitan centers.

How can we explain the apparent links between place of origin and socio-economic roots in Brazil and destination city in the United States? Once again, the key seems to lie in the sequencing of migration by social class, a phenomenon that is particularly important in a relatively small community like Governador Valadares that has a long tradition of emigration to the United States. In such cases, long-term migration patterns make for strong ties between the sending community and the destination city(ies) abroad. New immigrants from the community are likely to go to "familiar" United States cities; those where relatives or friends already have settled. This would explain, for example, the presence of several thousand Valadarenses in Danbury, Connecticut—a small city unfamiliar to most Brazilians. And it would also account for Brazilians from the tiny town of Tiros in southern Minas Gerais who have flocked to Long Branch, New Jersey, a place not much larger than their hometown. Or consider the Brazilian enclave in Cliffside, New Jersey just across the Hudson River from Manhattan. Most immigrants there are from Batinga, a small speck on the map in southern Bahia, a state in northeastern Brazil.

Thus, immigrants from sending communities like Governador Valadares or Tiros who establish roots in a locale abroad facilitate the migration of subsequent hometown immigrants. And this, in turn, has important implications for the social class of aspiring travelers. A fairly wide range of social classes are represented among Valadarenses in the United States. As one native told me, "all classes of Valadarenses are going to the United States from the rich to the poor." While perhaps an exaggeration, estimates suggest that about 20 percent the town's international migrants have working class origins, the result of a culture of out-migration that exposes citizens from diverse economic and educational backgrounds to the discourse on emigration. This discourse, coupled with the money sent back from relatives who already have emigrated to the United States, enable still more native sons and daughters to try their luck abroad. In short, in a town like Governador Valadares a culture of out-migration provides both the ideology and the material underpinnings—in the form of remittances from relatives in the United States—that make emigration possible for individuals from a range of social backgrounds.

People of modest means, then, people who in other circumstances could never hope to emigrate abroad, turn into international migrants with the financial help of family members who migrated earlier. In this way, a pervasive culture of out-migration enhances the emigration prospects of poorer, less educated segments of the population, with the result that Valadarenses in the United States appear to have more diverse antecedents than emigrants from other regions of Brazil. Finally, this explains the presence of a working class component in the Brazilian immigrant population of American cities where Valadarenses cluster—Boston, Newark, Danbury—but not in New York which tends to attract "big city" immigrants from Brazil.

Hometowns, Stereotypes, and Social Class

Although the origins of Brazilian immigrants in New York City are mixed,[1] if you were to ask the average Brazilian about his or her compatriots in the United States, the response would be something like: "Oh, those *mineiros*. They're the ones who go to the United States. It's a wonder that there are any people left in the whole state of Minas Gerais!" In Brazil and among Brazilian populations in the United States *mineiros* are seen as quintessential migrants. Indeed, natives of the state were pioneers in the Brazilian diaspora and dominated many Brazilian communities in the United States, particularly in the 1980s during the first years of the exodus.

If *mineiros* are occasionally lauded as pioneers, they are more often vilified for a variety of real or imagined sins by their compatriots from other parts of Brazil. *Mineiros* are the butt of endless jokes, and natives of the state are the victims of unflattering stereotypes. They are said to be very provincial; they are described as unrefined rubes especially in comparison to their cosmopolitan brethren from Rio de Janeiro and São Paulo. They are also said to be crafty, exploitative and mercenary and more than willing to take advantage of their fellow Brazilians for monetary gain.

The anti-mineiro sentiment expressed in New York's Brazilian immigrant community likely is rooted in geographical and rural-urban distinctions brought from home. What we are seeing here is a revamping and updating of the traditional discourse of urban Brazilians, especially those from major metropolitan areas like Rio de Janeiro and São Paulo, who have a long tradition of maligning people from the interior of their country, calling them unlettered *caboclos*, *caipiras* or *sertanejos* (hillbillies, hicks, or backwoodsmen).

Let me provide a few examples of some similar, albeit class-based, stereotypes current among Brazilians in the United States. Some members of the Brazilian elite[2] in New York refer to West 46th Street, "Little Brazil"—the midtown Manhattan street lined

---

1. About 80 percent were from cities in just two Brazilian states: Minas Gerais and Rio de Janeiro and most of the remainder were from urban areas of São Paulo, Paraná, and Espirito Santo, all in south central and southern Brazil, the relatively prosperous part of the nation.
2. The Brazilian elite is comprised of executives who run the city's Brazilian banks, airlines and corporations and their families.

with stores and businesses catering to Brazilian immigrants and tourists alike—as the *"baixada,"* a miserable swampy, impoverished, crime-ridden zone just outside the city of Rio de Janeiro. Calling Little Brazil by the name of what is arguably the most horrific place in Brazil reveals the disdain that some of the New York's elite Brazilians evince towards their immigrant compatriots. It also validates the social chasm that exists between themselves and Little Brazil's merchants who, although successful in business, generally come from fairly modest backgrounds in Brazil.

A similar story is told in the Brazilian community in Boston (Martes 1995b). An American nun was talking with an employee of the Brazilian Consulate in that city. When she heard that the consular employee lived in Brighton, she asked: "Do you know many Brazilians there?" The woman responded, "Here, my dear, we don't have Brazilians; we only have illiterates." Later when this woman introduced the American nun to her friend, she presented her as a Brazilian. "But I'm not Brazilian," the nun said. The woman was surprised. "You're not Brazilian? Then how did you learn to speak such excellent Portuguese?" The nun responded: "I learned it from the illiterates in northeastern Brazil."

Whatever the origin of these regional and socio-economic stereotypes, their existence reminds us that immigrant communities should not be blithely depicted as harmonious ethnic groups, nor should we assume a romanticized conception of ethnic solidarity that is often portrayed in the literature. In other words, we should not ignore differences in origin, social class, education, race, time of arrival in the United States and legal status, variants that may divide rather than unite immigrant communities (Pessar 1995).

Just one example: the varying times of arrival in the United States of immigrants from the same country can lead to rancorous divisions within an immigrant community. I found this to be true among Brazilians in New York City and research among other immigrant populations—Brazilians in Boston, Central Americans in Washington D.C. and Salvadorans on Long Island—confirms it (Martes 1996; Pessar 1995; Mahler 1995). Newly arrived, unseasoned immigrants are sometimes exploited, or at least, ignored by their compatriots who emigrated earlier. For example, I was told that oldtimers in New York's Brazilian immigrant community do not help newcomers with advice about jobs and housing, "they just pass along the suffering." Some immigrants also directed their ire at well-established Brazilians who, having lived in New York for decades, now own prosperous businesses in the city. They are loathe, claim their critics, to assist "greenhorn" Brazilians, seeing them as a potential source of future competition. Further evidence of the split between old and new immigrants comes from reports that more experienced immigrants sometimes demand that their newly arrived countrymen and women pay them "finder's fees" for telling them about available jobs (Martes 1996; Pessar 1995).

These examples suggest that the conditions that are often taken for granted among immigrant groups—ethnic solidarity and strong social support networks—sometimes do not exist or exist only in attenuated form in certain immigrant communities. Thus, we should not take ethnic unity among immigrant populations as a given, but rather consider the factors that either enhance or inhibit its development.

Among the factors that may inhibit a sense of solidarity within an immigrant community are the burdensome financial demands placed on new immigrants. An anthropologist who studied Hispanic immigrants points out the tremendous pressure they are under to earn a lot of money in a short period of time. They not only have to meet daily expenses, they may also have to pay off debts incurred for their travel to the United States and send remittances to relatives, not to mention saving money for their own return home. Such pressures "lead to the suspension of many social ties that conditioned life before migration. These immigrants thus come to the United States expecting to find their old community solidarity, but encounter a competitive, aggressive sub-culture instead" (Mahler 1995:30). Then, too, in cases where immigrant communities are divided along class lines, class interests often overpower ethnic solidarity. "Ethnicity becomes relevant and significant when class interests coincide," concludes a researcher who studied Korean immigrants in this country (Yoon 1991:317).

VITAL STATISTICS

Aside from social class, race, education and hometown origin, what else characterizes this immigration stream? While I have detailed data only on the Brazilian immigrants in New York City, there is reason to believe that their profile, except where specifically noted, is similar to those in other parts of the United States. Today, for example, there are only slightly more men than women in New York's Brazilian community, although during the first years of immigration in the mid-1980s, evidence suggests that men accounted for perhaps seventy percent of the immigrant population. A similar imbalance in the ratio of men to women also existed at the start of this migration surge in Boston and other cities with Brazilian immigrant enclaves.

The Brazilian population in New York City is quite young. Nearly forty percent of the Brazilians I studied are under thirty years old, while a slightly higher percentage are between thirty and forty; only five percent are over fifty. Children comprise a relatively small segment of New York's Brazilian immigrant population but their numbers are increasing. The greater presence of children, in turn, is related to the growing number of married immigrants. Sixty percent of the immigrants in my study were single when they came to New York, about one-quarter were married, and the rest were separated, divorced or widowed, but many immigrants married after coming to the United States.

Most married couples live together in New York. The pattern of one spouse remaining behind in the country of origin while the other seeks his or her fortune abroad and sends money home is uncommon among Brazilian immigrants in the city. But, it is somewhat more frequent among immigrants from Governador Valadares. Perhaps one-third of the small community of Valadarenses in New York are single or divorced women with children being cared for by relatives in Brazil or men who send remittances to their spouses and/or children back home. These same arrangements are also more prevalent in some other Brazilian enclaves in the United States, especially those with many Valadarenses.

This pattern is likely related to the socio-economic class and financial resources of immigrants and their families prior to their departure from Brazil. That is, if financially able, married couples usually travel to the United States together, but the families of those who have difficulty paying for the trip stay behind in Brazil. As a result, single and divorced mothers with children in the care of relatives in Brazil and married men with families there were described to me in similar terms; they were called "money machines" and the "bankers" of their relatives back home.

AMONG FAMILY

When they arrive in New York even unmarried immigrants or those whose spouses and children stayed in Brazil may have relatives in the city. Indeed, the more recent arrivals have come to the United States via chain migration, a process through which new immigrants are brought to the host country with the help—financial and otherwise—of relatives or friends who are already there. One immigrant is followed by others, with additional immigrants bringing with them ties of kinship and friendship to still more people back home. Those in the sending community, in turn, have ever expanding networks in the destination locale. Migrant streams become self-perpetuating after they start to flow because migration becomes easier as each new immigrant lessens the cost of later migration for a network of relatives and friends. And with reduced costs, still more people are enticed to try their luck abroad, creating still more links between sending and receiving communities (Massey 1988).

Among the Brazilians I studied, the longer immigrants had been in New York, usually the more relatives they had helped bring to the city. Some had sponsored dozens of family members—siblings, cousins, parents, nieces, nephews, even in-laws—while others had also aided close friends. One Brazilian who had lived in New York for over a decade told me that he had helped so many family members come to the city that he had lost count. Another long-time resident had sponsored her four siblings, their spouses and innumerable nieces and nephews.

Chain migration typically involves more than just assistance in funding the trip. There are many advantages to having a network of family and friends in an unfamiliar city like New York. Already settled relatives can reduce the cost of the newcomer's first days or weeks by providing a place to stay and giving advice on transportation and other aspects of city living. They can help locate work through personal contacts or knowledge of the job market. And when newly arrived Brazilian immigrants speak of their *saudades*, their deep longing for their native land, there is no one like a close relative to soothe the sting of loneliness during their early days in an alien metropolis. Thus, kin can diminish the costs of migration, both material and emotional, in many ways.

This, then, is a broadly painted portrait of Brazilian immigrants in New York City. They are mostly middle class and fairly well educated and many come from large cities in Brazil. Nevertheless, as we will see in the chapter to follow, the niche Brazilian immigrants occupy in the city's labor market reflects neither their antecedents nor their abilities. Because they are new immigrants, many of whom lack English skills and work papers, they find themselves on the lowest rung of New York's employment ladder.

3

Working New York

Brazilian immigrants clean houses, offices and hotel rooms, take care of kids and walk dogs. They drive radio cabs and limousines. They dance in gogo bars and shine shoes and they sell books and food on the city's sidewalks. They bus tables, wash dishes and deliver pizzas. They paint and renovate apartments and houses and do landscaping in the suburbs. Since Brazilians are in the United States to earn money, they take whatever jobs are available to newcomers in this country who have little knowledge of English and no work papers. In short, despite the educational level of Brazilian immigrants, language and legal status determine their niche in the labor market.

Before exploring the actual work that Brazilian immigrants do, it is important to understand where the labor of Brazilians and other recent immigrants in the city fits into New York's complex job market. To do that we must look beyond the city and adopt a global perspective on immigration. Evidence suggests that U.S. employers seeking low-cost labor either find it in low-wage countries abroad—the path taken by many American manufacturing firms—or they use cheap imported labor in the form of immigrant workers. Unlike manufacturers, businesses in the service sector of the economy have to follow the latter course because services require local labor—restaurants need busboys and dishwashers, motels need chambermaids, and companies that clean offices need a janitorial staff. Since these businesses obviously cannot export themselves, many come to rely on low-cost imported labor.

The need for such labor is especially acute in cities like New York, Washington and Los Angeles that have major service industries (Repak 1995). Still, a debate exists about what is causing the rise in demand for immigrant workers in these cities. Some researchers argue that the number of low-wage service jobs has increased significantly in recent years; the more jobs, the greater the demand for workers to fill them (Sassen-Koob 1986). Others suggest immigrants have found this type of employment, not because there are more jobs per se, but because service sector jobs are being abandoned by many who traditionally held them (Waldinger 1989; 1996).

Each side of the debate can be outlined as follows. In certain cities like New York, jobs in the low-wage service sector are burgeoning because of the expanded presence of high income individuals there. The needs of the wealthy and the upper-middle class, the top 20 percent of the population with considerable discretionary income, have fueled the growth of personal service jobs like live-in nannies and other domestic servants, dog walkers, drivers, restaurant workers, caterers, beauticians, manicurists and the like. These high income earners are upper level managers and professionals employed in New York's banking, investment, trading, communications and advertising industries. These same industries also create their own market for low-wage, low skill jobs—for office cleaners, stock clerks, and messengers.

In short, low-wage workers are required to service the household needs and elaborate consumption patterns of an expanding high income elite. As such, the growth of work in services leads to a more bifurcated job structure. On one side is the demand for workers willing to take low paying, low status unstable jobs that generally appeal only to those with few or no alternatives, like new immigrants. On the other, there is the demand for high-skilled and highly paid executives, managers and professionals who inhabit the upper reaches of the city's corporate structure.

Other researchers argue, however, that it is changes in the labor supply that explain the increased demand for immigrant workers. Here the reasoning is that as the proportion of white workers has declined in cities like New York and Los Angeles, a "vacancy chain" has been set in motion that allows non-whites and some immigrants to move up the job ladder (Waldinger 1989:221). Immigrants, at least initially, are replacement labor. Over time they carve out their own occupational niches, developing channels of labor market information, support, and recruitment.

WHY IMMIGRANTS?

Whatever its specific cause, a demand exists for cheap immigrant labor in New York and other cities with burgeoning service sectors. The crucial question is: Why immigrants? This has become a contentious issue in recent years with a few researchers and many politicians and political pundits asserting that immigrants, particularly undocumented aliens, are taking jobs that would otherwise be filled by citizens, or at least by legal residents of this country (Brimelow 1995; Briggs and Moore 1994). Is this true? Are newcomers *really* taking jobs that would be held by Americans, including members of native-born minority groups?

In order to answer this question, we must look at the nature of the low-wage service sector jobs that employ new immigrants. One of the key attributes of these jobs is the ease with which workers holding them are replaced. As a result, employers have scant interest in maintaining a stable labor force and this, in turn, makes for short-term jobs with little or no security and meager hope of advancement. High labor turnover also reflects the premium that many service sector employers place on a flexible work force; one that expands and contracts as the need warrants. Flexibility is an integral part of many low-wage service jobs because they are not unionized. This allows a work environment in which employers can control workers in direct and, at times, arbitrary ways. Workers in such jobs can be dismissed with little cause or their work shifts can be changed without notice.

Then, of course, there is the low rate of pay and the absence of fringe benefits that characterize this work. Many service sector jobs pay the minimum wage or just above or a worker's income varies a good deal because it depends largely on tips. Moreover low-wage service jobs are often done under difficult working conditions; they may involve considerable physical labor and work at odd hours, like nights and weekends.

Finally, some substantial but unknown portion of low-wage service jobs belong to the informal economy. Jobs in the informal economy are unregulated in terms of working conditions, wage and hour laws, and taxes withheld. The informal sector is big business in a city like New York; estimates suggest that 39 *billion* dollars in legal, unreported economic activity took place in the city in 1993 alone (Sontag 1993)! It is no surprise that informal sector jobs are the ones *least* likely to demand work papers or otherwise require immigrants to document their legal status.

Restaurant work illustrates most of the conditions that characterize low-wage service employment. Jobs washing dishes in steamy kitchens and busing heavy loads of dirty dishes—work typically done by new immigrants—require little English, minimal skill and the workers doing them are easily replaced. Employees are often called on to work nights and weekends and full-service restaurants usually have two shifts of workers whose numbers vary according to the time of day and the season of the year. Seasonal layoffs are not uncommon. Turnover in these jobs is generally high as low wages, lack of benefits, sometimes grueling conditions and few opportunities for advancement sap worker morale.

All of this points to one stark fact: low-wage service jobs are undesirable by almost any standard. They are jobs that people with other employment options simply reject. So the question then becomes: Who would *want* such jobs? Not Americans, argue some researchers, including those from native disadvantaged groups (Briggs and Moore 1994; Fix and Passel 1994). New immigrants, however, especially those without papers, have few alternatives and thus become "ideal" workers from the vantage point of employers. Frankly, immigrants—and again, most particularly undocumented immigrants—have less power than native-born workers. Immigrants are less likely to challenge poor working conditions, long hours at substandard wages and abrupt firings. They are much more likely than American workers "to go along to get along." After all, what are their options? Other low-wage jobs under similarly difficult conditions?

This is why new immigrants—with or without work papers— are welcomed with open arms by many low-wage employers, be they the owners of chic Manhattan restaurants looking for dishwashers or harried career women in need of nannies to care for their children or immigrant entrepreneurs seeking seamstresses for their sweatshops.[1] Take certain jobs in domestic service as an

---

1. It is estimated that half of the 22,000 sewing shops in the United States break labor laws and thus constitute "sweatshops" (Adelson 1996).

example. A long-term nanny in New York City had this to say about her pivotal role:

> "We could close down the city...If there's a garbage strike, the trash just lies there. If there's a postal strike, the mail doesn't get delivered. But if the nannies were to strike it would be different. You can't just leave a baby around until there's someone ready to take care of it" (quoted in Cheever 1995:87).

Since recent immigrants constitute a large, pliant labor force with few employment opportunities, their absence would either mean higher labor costs or low-wage service jobs that went begging. For this reason, it is difficult to deny the assertion that a slice of the American economy is "hooked on" undocumented immigrant labor.

Does the presence of cheap, docile immigrant labor adversely affect native workers as is commonly thought? Most economists agree that in the short run immigrants who work for cheap wages can depress pay in low-skilled jobs. Nevertheless, there is little evidence that immigrants have a sizeable or long-term effect on wage structure. For example, the Mariel boatlift which saw an influx of 125,000 unskilled workers in the city of Miami—7 percent of the total labor force—had no demonstrable effect on the unemployment rate or wage levels of unskilled non-Hispanic workers there. In short, wage growth and decline for both skilled and unskilled jobs appear to be unrelated to immigration. New immigrants, in fact, appear to have a negative effect on the labor market opportunities of only one group: immigrants who immediately preceded them (Wright 1995; Butcher and Card 1991; Fix and Passel 1994).

The one area in which new immigrants can have a negative impact on Americans, especially native minority groups, is in hiring. Evidence suggests that for some jobs immigrant employment networks are the key to new hires who are likely to come from within the immigrant community itself. While networks benefit employers by supplying them with a stable pool of inexpensive labor and lowering recruitment and training costs, they also tend to shut out members of American minority groups from the hiring process (Waldinger 1993).

We can see how this works in one low-wage Brazilian immigrant employment enclave: shoeshining. Brazilians have a near monopoly on jobs shining shoes in shoe repair shops and kiosks around Manhattan. As such, all of the Brazilian shoeshiners in my study found their jobs through word of mouth in the Brazilian community. While shining shoes does not require much training, new immigrants need some familiarity with the techniques and products of the trade; this they get from fellow Brazilians the first day on the job. It is obvious, then, why such immigrant networks are useful to employers; they can reduce the cost of hiring and training new workers to virtually zero.

HARD AT WORK

If low-wage service sector jobs are so undesirable, why do Brazilians or other recent immigrants even *want* them? The answer is unambiguous: the key attraction of such jobs is that they pay considerably more money than the newcomers were earning back home. Brazilian immigrants in New York City earn at least $6.00 an hour, somewhat more than the federal minimum wage (Klintowitz 1996). Some domestic servants as well as the few Brazilians working in renovation and construction make $10 or $12 an hour—although much less than union scale for similar jobs—still an impressive sum by Brazilian standards.

To understand just how attractive U.S. wages are even in low paying jobs, all we have to do is compare them to the earnings of Brazilian immigrants before they left home. Consider the fact that in 1995 in Brazil's six largest cities the average salary was just under $500 a month and the per capita income for the nation as a whole was only one-fifth that of the United States. As a result, even though many of the new immigrants were employed in Brazil in professional or semi-professional positions that paid good salaries by local standards, they are meager in comparison to what they earn in the United States, even in the type of low-wage service jobs discussed above.

A few examples of what Brazilians were earning before and after they came to the United States illustrate this point. One woman whose salary had been only $200 a month as head nurse in a big city hospital in Brazil was making nearly five times as much as a babysitter in New York, while another immigrant who was paid $500 a month as a mechanical engineer in Brazil earned $400 a week working as a private chauffeur in New York. In dozens of similar examples given to me by Brazilian immigrants in the city, differences in the rates of pay were typically four to one; one month's earnings in Brazil were the equivalent of one week's pay in the United States.

While low-wage jobs in the United States seem lucrative to those accustomed to Brazilian pay scales, do recent immigrants even receive the minimum wage? What about all the news accounts that suggest that new immigrants, especially those without work papers, often receive sub-standard wages? Evidence suggests that not too many undocumented immigrants earn less than the legal minimum wage with two major exceptions: agriculture and the apparel industry—neither of which employ Brazilians. I encountered no Brazilians, for example, working anything like the exhausting 60-hour-a-week regime for only $600 to $800 a month that has been reported for undocumented Chinese immigrants in New York City (Kwong 1994).

Even if employers of low-wage service workers usually pay the minimum wage or somewhat above, many still benefit financially because they often pay "off the books." By skirting the law and failing to pay social security taxes, unemployment compensation and other fringe benefits, employers can save thousands of dollars annually.

Just who works off the books? The legal status of the worker seems to be less important than the type of job held. Certain jobs, like those in domestic service and shoeshining usually are part of the informal economy, that is, they are "off the books," while restaurant work ordinarily is not. Yet, it is also true that undocumented Brazilians are more likely than legal immigrants[2] to work as maids, babysitters, shoeshiners, street vendors and in other typical off-the-books employment. Even Brazilians working on the books rarely receive benefits of any kind. "Health insurance? What's that?" joked one Brazilian immigrant with a slightly bitter edge in her voice. The failure to pay overtime and the absence of worker's compensation for those injured on the job are particular sources of irritation in the immigrant community.

---

2. A legal immigrant has a green card, a document issued by the U.S. Immigration Service that gives the non-citizen the right to paid employment.

Conventional wisdom has it that while immigrants do not earn much or receive any benefits while working under often arduous conditions, their situation is not as unfair as it seems because they do not pay income or social security taxes. This is part of the image—now much in vogue—of the immigrant as "freeloader" who receives more than she or he contributes to American society. While I lack data on this for Brazilian immigrants, research on other immigrant groups questions this assumption. For example, one study of undocumented Mexican women found that nearly three-quarters of them worked "on the books" and had both social security and income taxes withheld from their wages; only those employed as domestic servants and paid in cash did not. Another study of undocumented immigrants from several countries living in the New York area came up with similar findings. Nearly all the immigrants had paid social security taxes and about 70 percent had also paid state and federal income taxes (Simon and DeLey 1986; Papademetriou and DiMarzio 1986). An interesting question in this regard and one that is never asked in the discussions about "freeloaders" is: What happens to all the money that immigrants pay into social security but never collect because they leave the country before retirement?

MAKING ENDS MEET

How do immigrants in low-wage jobs manage to make ends meet in an expensive city like New York and still save money for the return home? The answer is two-fold: hard work and shared expenses. By working long hours, often nights and weekends, Brazilian immigrants are able to earn what they regard as good money. For example, drivers of radio call cars willing to work 12-hour shifts, 6 days a week can take home $500, a considerable sum by Brazilian standards. Or, by working many hours and cleaning at least two apartments a day, an immigrant can earn $500 or even $600 a week, although $300 to $400 is more typical. The income of busboys also can reach $500 a week for those willing to put in the hours, and the few Brazilians who work as waiters earn still more. Even street vendors—the lowest paid Brazilian immigrants—can take home $250 to $300 for an arduous seven-day work week. The majority of Brazilians in New York

City probably earn somewhere between $1000 and $2000 a month, but the combined income of couples is often much higher. For example, a married couple working together can net up to $4000 a month cleaning at least two apartments or houses a day since taxes and social security are rarely withheld for domestic jobs.

Some Brazilian immigrants make up for their low-wages by working two jobs, including a fair number with two full-time jobs. Almost a quarter of the immigrants I studied were holding more than one job at the time I interviewed them. Restaurants are the most common source of second jobs because their work hours are usually flexible and often involve nights and weekends. Immigrants with two jobs led truly frantic lives doing little but traveling back and forth to work and home again to catch a few hours of sleep.

Chico, a former high school teacher in Rio de Janeiro, was employed in two full-time jobs six days a week. He awoke at 6:30 AM, and took the subway from Queens to Manhattan to begin work by 7:15 at a shoeshine shop near Penn Station. He shined shoes for the next eleven hours and then caught the subway to Greenwich Village where he began his 6:00 evening shift as a dishwasher in a restaurant. He worked almost non-stop in the restaurant's kitchen until 11:00 PM and then exhausted, boarded the subway back to Queens. On Sunday, his one day off, he slept, did the laundry and wrote letters to his family in Brazil.

Aside from hard work, Brazilian immigrants also try to make ends meet and still save money by minimizing expenses, which they do in several ways. Since rent is their most costly budget item, the vast majority share living quarters with friends or relatives, dividing not only the cost of rent but also utilities and telephone. Then, too, it is not uncommon for married couples to take in boarders to help defray expenses. Brazilian immigrants also spend as little as possible on household items. Since they view their stay in New York as temporary, why put much money into furniture or household goods they will not be able to take home with them to Brazil?

Frugality also plays a role in the personal attire of some New York Brazilians who are unwilling, especially at first, to spend money on winter clothes. Their reasoning is the same: Why waste hard earned dollars on heavy coats, sweaters and boots when they will soon be escaping New York's frosty clime and heading back to their sunny homeland. Yet winter in the city requires proper dress if only a warm coat, scarf and gloves. A few Brazilian immigrants have a cost-free solution to this apparel dilemma; they pick up an assortment of donated used clothing from a social service agency in Queens that otherwise caters to the city's needy and homeless.

Brazilian immigrants also are careful about what they spend on entertainment, not a difficult issue given the long hours they work and the little time most have for leisure activities anyway. This is particularly true during the first months in New York when many new immigrants turn into fanatical money-making machines whose entire existence is caught up in saving for the return home. "Leisure is very costly here," they say, because it takes time from working, and less work means less money. And, in an expensive city like New York, going to the movies, concerts, bars and restaurants can swallow up a lot of dollars that otherwise might end up in a savings account.

Time for a Change

Given the low pay and dead end nature of the work most Brazilian immigrants do, it is no surprise that they are not tied to their jobs and change them often. This was a source of some frustration during my research when I went to a restaurant or a shoe repair shop to locate Brazilians I had interviewed in the past only to find that my former interviewees had vanished in thin air and other Brazilians were working in their place. Immigrants continually hop from job to job as they look for better wages, hours and working conditions. For example, over the eight months I tracked the dizzying career path of one Brazilian immigrant he was a part-time handyman, street vendor, shoeshiner, homecare attendant, bakery store clerk, and radio call car driver. My own experience confirmed the observation of another immigrant who suggested that if I were to wait one year and then return to the place of work of all the Brazilians who had been part of my original study, I would be lucky to encounter even one or two of them since nearly all would have moved on to different jobs.

For immigrants to change jobs so often, other jobs must be available, which raises the controversial issue of the employment

CHAPTER 3 • WORKING NEW YORK • 53

of undocumented immigrants. Recall that about half of the Brazilians in my study were undocumented. In 1986 the U.S. Congress passed the Immigration Reform and Control Act known as IRCA, the primary aim of which was to stem the flow of undocumented aliens entering the United States by making it unlawful for employers to hire them.[3] The rationale behind this legislation was that by subjecting employers to fines of up to $2000 for hiring undocumented workers—those without proper papers—jobs for such workers would dry up. Then, without the magnet of jobs, undocumented immigrants would return to their native lands and others would be discouraged from coming to this country.

Things did not turn out this way. Despite some initial success, it is generally agreed that IRCA cut the flow of undocumented immigrants far less than expected. Although the ban on hiring undocumented workers may have made it more difficult for them to find jobs, it certainly did not stem the tide of illegal entry (Bean, Edmonston, and Passel 1992; Golden 1991; Kilborn 1993). One reason for this failure is clear. While there are somewhat fewer jobs for undocumented workers than before IRCA was passed, the economic conditions back home that propelled Brazilians and other immigrants to come to this country in the first place remain largely unchanged. As a result, there is no evidence that immigrants became so discouraged by the effects of IRCA that they simply gave up and went home. In one study of the law's impact, not a single immigrant questioned knew anyone who had left the United States because IRCA had made it harder to get a job (Repak 1995).

My own and similar research suggests that the recession of the late 1980s and early 1990s and the subsequent loss of low-wage service jobs had a greater impact on the employment of Brazilians and other immigrants than IRCA's threat of sanctions against employers who hire undocumented workers (Repak 1995). While some employers do indeed require workers to show firm proof that they are "legal," most simply ask to see a social security card. This is easy enough to arrange since, for $150 or less, a social secu-

---

3. The other major provision of IRCA was the Amnesty Program. This was intended to legalize long-term undocumented immigrants, defined as those who had resided continually in the United States since 1982.

rity card can be obtained in one of the thriving markets for counterfeit documents that exist in New York and other U.S. cities with large immigrant populations (Suro 1990).

Still, it would be wrong to assume that IRCA has had no effect at all. IRCA's impact on immigrant employment has varied by job category, so the legislation seems to have affected male and female immigrants somewhat differently. Domestic service, which is nearly all-female, was little touched by the law. Aside from a few high profile cases involving the domestic servants of politicians and political appointees, IRCA has done nothing to reduce the demand for such workers. The legislation is virtually unenforceable for household employees anyway. Employers rarely ask to see the work papers of housecleaners, baby sitters and nannies and are even less likely to fire those already in their employ who do not have them. IRCA also has had no notable impact on certain jobs held primarily by men—shoeshining and odd jobs in landscaping, painting and renovation. But IRCA did make a difference in other employment categories dominated by male immigrants. In Washington DC, for example, of the few undocumented immigrants who said that they lost their jobs as the result of IRCA, most were men who worked in the construction industry (Repak 1995).

Employers continue to hire undocumented workers not only because IRCA's sanctions against doing so have not been aggressively enforced, but because in a number of areas the demand for cheap labor is not being met by native workers or even by legal immigrants. Moreover, for some employers the financial benefits of hiring off-the-book workers outweigh the cost of possible sanctions (Mahler 1995). In other words, some employers are so desperate for low-wage workers that it matters little whether those hired are documented or not.

A few examples of the flouting of IRCA's sanctions: About half of the restaurant owners interviewed in one study in Washington DC admitted that even after the passage of IRCA they retained employees without documents. Most said that they had "no choice" because of a severe labor shortage in the area (Repak 1995). In New York City, the refrain was the same. "I can't hire all legal people," said the owner of a sweatshop in Manhattan after it was raided by agents of the U.S. Immigration and Naturalization Service. "Who wants to work in this dirty job? American people?

No," she maintained. The owner of another garment factory also was frank about why he employed undocumented immigrants. "Let me tell you honestly. I think I have to hire illegal people because I don't want to pay $7, $8 for work that illegal people can do for $4.25" (quoted in Dugger 1996).

Employers sometimes collude with undocumented workers in skirting the law by telling them where they can buy counterfeit work papers and social security cards so that they can be hired "legally." This is particularly true in those industries that historically have relied on cheap illegal immigrant labor. If low labor costs are foremost, then complying with the law is relatively simple: a document, any document will do since employers are under no legal obligation to check the validity of the "work papers" shown to them.

JUST WHAT DO THEY DO?

Legal or otherwise, Brazilian immigrants get jobs. They can usually find work cleaning apartments, caring for children, shining shoes, washing dishes or busing tables with little more than a reference from a friend or relative. Since coming to the United States, the one hundred Brazilians in my study had been employed in a total of three hundred and twenty-five jobs, for an average of 3.25 jobs apiece. Women had worked in fewer job categories than men largely because the great majority of immigrant women in New York had been employed at one time or another in a single job classification—domestic service. In fact, four out of five Brazilian women in my study had worked as live-in housekeepers, day maids, nannies and/or babysitters. No single job category employed nearly as high a proportion of men. The only one that came close was restaurant work which comprised 30 percent of total male employment. But both men and women had worked in a wider range of jobs than expected, some of which, like school teaching, banking and retail sales, are not usually associated with immigrants. This reflects the fact that while my study population was mostly comprised of new immigrants, more than 10 percent had lived in New York for a decade or more. As relatively "old-timers," some had ascended the employment ladder and no longer held jobs typical of recent immigrants. The major job categories in which Brazilian immigrants are employed are profiled below.

Keeping House in New York

Over the last two decades the demand for household workers has expanded dramatically in the greater New York area and elsewhere in the United States. The transformation of the middle class housewife-mother into a full-time, salaried employee has meant that housework and, in some cases, child care have been given over to paid domestics (Margolis 1984). The nature of domestic service also has changed in recent years. Today household servants are more likely to come in to clean once or twice a week or to work for companies like Merry Maids than to be employed full-time by a single family (Johnston 1995). Despite these changes, the long American tradition of the immigrant domestic continues. Although New York is not yet like Los Angeles or San Diego, cities in which domestic work has become an occupation done almost exclusively by undocumented female labor, housecleaning and child care are by far the most important sources of employment for undocumented Brazilian women (Mydans 1991).

We tend to think of domestic service as an all-female occupation and women do indeed dominate it among Brazilian immigrants in New York City, but a few Brazilian men also are employed in this job category. About thirteen percent of the male immigrants I interviewed had done domestic work at some point since coming to this country. They cleaned houses or worked as butlers, valets or chauffeurs. Some of these men were part of a married pair jointly employed as domestics in a single household. Hired by affluent families in the New York metropolitan area, such couples usually lived in the homes of their employers. The woman was usually charged with cooking, cleaning, and child care, while her husband served as the family butler, gardener and/or chauffeur.

Domestic work done by immigrant women encompasses two distinct jobs: live-in housekeeper and day maid. Live-in domestic servants live and work in the homes of their employees, while day maids or housecleaners have their own residences and typically clean a number of apartments on a rotating schedule. Living-in has both major benefits and serious costs. Live-in jobs are particularly well suited to immigrants who have just arrived in the United States. Such employment not only provides a cost-free place to live with no commuting expenses, but also, the new immigrant does not have to worry about arranging for telephone or utilities or learning how to use public transportation. And, with living expenses held to a minimum, newcomers are able to save quite a lot of money in a short period of time. Even at the lower end of the pay scale, a frugal live-in can put away $1000 to $1500 a month. For all these reasons, live-in housekeeping is often the first job a woman has when she comes to New York. Half of the Brazilian women I interviewed had worked as live-ins, most soon after they arrived in this country.

The major disadvantage of these positions is their vast potential for exploitation. Living-in is seldom an eight-hour a day job; some families expect live-ins to be at their beck and call at all times except on their days off. As such, live-ins may lack lives of their own and become isolated from the rest of the immigrant community. One Brazilian told me how six days a week her life was a continual maelstrom of cooking, cleaning, doing the laundry and caring for a rambunctious three-year old. The live-in's job is never done because her home and place of work are the same.

Despite its drawbacks, however, a few Brazilian women consider the ordeal of life as a live-in worth the price because it can provide a rare opportunity to qualify for a green card. Recall that a green card is that much sought after item that turns an undocumented immigrant into a legal resident alien who has the right to live and work in this country. Under U.S. immigration law, housework and child care are among the few jobs that permit employers to sponsor immigrants for green cards, making domestic service one of the only ways that women without relatives in the United States can legalize their status. The law requires immigrant women to have had prior child care experience since most of those being sponsored for green cards take care of young children, while sponsoring families must demonstrate a moderately high income.

The system is ripe for abuse. Once the papers are filed, it takes at least two years and $3000 or more in legal fees before a green card is issued. During this time immigrant women are in legal limbo, bound to their current employers and without other job options. No matter what the conditions of employment, the promise of a green card is a powerful incentive to stay with the sponsoring family. In effect, then, immigration law helps mitigate the shortage of domestics in this country and dampens demands for state support of child care by providing a large pool of relatively cheap and docile workers to help meet the domestic needs of some high income American families (Colen 1990).

Except for those being sponsored for green cards, live-in domestic work is typically a brief stage in the lives of Brazilian immigrant women in New York City. After a few months or a year they leave the homes of their employers and rent apartments which they usually share with other immigrants. But most continue to work as housekeepers, baby sitters or nannies although now on a "live-out" basis. The ideal is to be employed at least five days a week by a few individuals or families, cleaning each apartment or house once or twice a week. For those willing to put in the hours, the work can pay quite well. In her research on Brazilian immigrants in Boston, Cristina Martes (1996) found that, of all immigrants, women doing housecleaning were earning the most consistent income and were best able to save money. She notes, for example, that a woman who cleans two houses a day at $50 a house, can take home $500 a week or $2000 a month, a very comfortable income by Brazilian standards.

Still, domestic service shares many of the disadvantages of other low-wage service jobs. It is hard work, for one. Women often told me how, after eight or nine hours of cleaning kitchens and bathrooms, washing floors, dusting, vacuuming, and doing several loads of laundry, they arrived home too exhausted to do anything but take to their beds. Domestic work also offers little job security. When individuals or families go away on holiday or summer vacation, the "cleaning lady" is not needed, and Brazilians complain about the uncertainty and seasonality of the work. Many said their income falls dramatically during the summer months. Others told of a sudden drop in pay when one employer or another deemed their apartments in less frequent need of cleaning, or worse still, that they could not afford a housekeeper's services at all. Moreover, those employed in housework and private child care almost never receive fringe benefits and their wages are nearly always paid off the books.

Such are the penalties that come with working in the informal economy. Still, other then shoe shining, street vending and some restaurant work, the only jobs employing large numbers of Brazilians that almost never require a green card are those in domestic service. To be sure, one has to know some English and have strong personal references, but these are easily supplied because domestic service jobs are passed back and forth between friends and relatives within the immigrant community. Despite IRCA and the tirades against "illegal aliens," then, New Yorkers looking for someone to clean an apartment or to care for their children rarely ask about a prospective employee's legal status. And, as Brazilian immigrants are quick to point out, most Americans have no idea what a green card looks like anyway!

Serving New York

"Would you like some fresh ground pepper on your Caesar salad?" inquires the food handler[4] in an upscale Manhattan restaurant. The chances are excellent that the employee asking this question is an immigrant and, very possibly, an undocumented immigrant at that. This was brought home to me one evening when I noticed that the service was unusually slow at a trendy new restaurant in one of New York's public parks. It is a full-service restaurant and waiters scuttled about, but oddly no busboys were there to assist them carry food trays or clear away dirty dishes. When I asked our waiter about this he said that the restaurant indeed had tried to hire busboys but could not find anyone to take these jobs because "they pay so little"—$2.00 an hour plus a percentage of the tips. The restaurant is owned by a large corporation that won a much publicized right to open in a public park by promising to charge moderate prices. Both its high profile and official connection to the city would make it unseemly, and probably risky, for the restaurant to hire undocumented immigrants for its low-wage positions. Hence, the absence of busboys. After

---

4. Food handlers in full-service restaurants deliver food and drinks to the table, waiters take food orders and busboys clear away dirty dishes. Full-service restaurants are distinguished from fast food restaurants by having table service and other amenities.

all, who but those with no other options would agree to work for such paltry wages?

This tale highlights the critical role immigrants play in the restaurant industry, the single most important source of employment in New York for *all* immigrants. In 1980, when immigrants made up 25 percent of the city's population, they accounted for 54 percent of restaurant workers and the proportion is almost certainly higher today. Moreover, restaurant work is one of the fastest growing job categories in the country. The number of restaurant workers has gone from 1.7 million in 1964 to 7.1 million in 1994, while the total U.S. work force had barely doubled (Bailey 1987; Johnston 1995). These figures are reflected in the employment profile of New York's Brazilian immigrant community, where restaurant work is to Brazilian men what domestic service is to Brazilian women. Nearly half of the men in my research sample worked in restaurants at one time or another since coming to New York, making restaurant work by far the largest source of male employment. Just as live-in domestic positions are common among Brazilian women when they are new to the city, one-third of the men in my study listed busboy or dishwasher as their first job.

Brazilians, like most recent immigrants, are hired for the unskilled and semi-skilled positions in full-service restaurants. But while busing tables and washing dishes are the most frequent restaurant jobs held by Brazilian immigrants, they are not the only ones. Food preparation and food service in upscale Manhattan restaurants involve many workers doing a variety of tasks. Aside from chefs and their assistants, there are kitchen cleaners, including dishwashers, salad makers who wash and prepare greens, waiters who recite the daily specials and take food and drink orders, food assemblers who carry completed orders from the kitchen and assemble them on trays, food handlers who set dishes before customers and dispense bread, fresh pepper and grated cheese, and busboys who fill water glasses and remove dirty dishes. There are also food buyers, restaurant managers, maitre'ds, bartenders, reservationists, coat checkers and rest room attendants. The last two are the only restaurant jobs in which Brazilian women are usually employed.

A sprinkling of Brazilian immigrants are found in nearly all these positions in New York restaurants and a few of them have managed to move up the job ladder. In fact, restaurants are the city's only industry employing large numbers of Brazilians that provide immigrants with any real opportunity for job mobility. Restaurant jobs lead upward from the bottom-ranked kitchen cleaner, through dishwasher, busboy, food assembler and handler to waiter. Waiting on tables is the top position held by most Brazilians employed in restaurants, although a few have made it to cook, bartender, food buyer, and maitre'd.

Some New York City restaurants have strong immigrant employment networks in which hiring is done almost exclusively through immigrant connections. Word of a job opening spreads rapidly among the restaurant's employees and a job seeker from the immigrant community is quickly found to take the position. New York's Brazilian immigrants dominate labor recruitment in several restaurants. One is a large midtown Manhattan restaurant featuring southwestern cuisine. On any given day about thirty Brazilians can be found working there as dishwashers, busboys, waiters, bartenders, cooks, hostesses, food buyers and the like. The first Brazilian was hired in the mid-1980s and over the years through word-of-mouth recruitment somewhere between two and three hundred Brazilians have found jobs there.

Once such immigrant employment networks are set up, they often become self-perpetuating, even branching out to new establishments. For example, when the owner of the restaurant mentioned above opened a second restaurant, it too was quickly staffed by friends and relatives of current Brazilian employees. The downside of such networks is that they can effectively exclude members of other ethnic and racial groups or other immigrant communities from finding employment in the labor market niches that such immigrant networks monopolize.

Driving New York

One image of New York that many visitors to the city retain long after they leave are the loudly honking, bright yellow taxicabs that cruise Manhattan streets in search of fares. Less well known, but equally important for transporting city residents are the fleets of radio call cars that ply New York's outer boroughs, particularly Queens and Brooklyn, picking up passengers who have phoned radio dispatchers requesting cars. This, too, is an immigrant-dominated industry and one in which many (male) Brazilians work. After restaurant work, driving a radio call car was the second most common job among the Brazilian immigrant men in my study.

Legally, radio call car drivers can only transport passengers who have phoned in requesting pick-ups. As such, all drivers are affiliated with car service companies that employ dispatchers to answer the calls and direct drivers to the addresses of waiting customers. Most Brazilian drivers work for one of the five car service companies owned by fellow Brazilians in Queens and these companies, in turn, employ mainly Brazilian drivers.

The life of a radio call car driver in New York City is not an easy one. In order to take home what they consider reasonable pay, Brazilian drivers must follow grueling twelve-hour-a-day, six-day-a-week schedules because their expenses are so high—fees to the car service company, insurance, gas, car repairs, and parking tickets. Moreover, driving a call car comes with an added worry not common to most jobs: crime. New York's tabloid press regularly carries stories about radio call car drivers—almost invariably male immigrants—being mugged or even murdered.

Despite these drawbacks many Brazilian men prefer driving radio call cars to other types of work. For one, it is a flexible job; a driver can make his own hours and be his own boss. It also pays quite well by Brazilian standards. A driver willing to put in a six-day week can regularly take home about $500. This work has another advantage. More than most jobs open to new immigrants, it conforms to middle class Brazilian norms of what constitutes "suitable" work. To be sure, driving a cab is not something an educated person in Brazil would do, but unlike domestic service and restaurant employment, it lacks the taint of manual labor. In Brazil working with one's hands is a badge of lower class status. This association is so strong that middle class Brazilians find their American counterpart's penchant for hobbies like gardening or carpentry very peculiar indeed. Brazil's "gentleman's complex," the ideology that denigrates manual labor and those who engage in it, is one that Brazilians do not easily shed even as immigrants (Freyre 1964; Wagley 1971).

Selling New York

The quintessential first job for Brazilians in New York City is street vending. Even more than live-in housekeeping and unskilled restaurant work, selling books, food and other items on the city's sidewalks is tailor-made for newcomers. It requires very little English—not much more than giving the price of one's wares. It is largely unregulated and it requires no documents, not even a social security card. Street selling is a gender neutral job, the only one that employs roughly equal numbers of female and male immigrants. But it is also a job that most immigrants leave behind as soon as they find employment elsewhere. My research suggests that more than 90 percent of Brazilian street vendors had been in New York less than six months and that a three or four month street-selling stint was typical before they moved on to other work.

Street vending is seen as undesirable for many reasons. For one, it requires work outdoors in all kinds of weather. Street vendors only pack up their wares and head home in heavy downpours, snowstorms, or when the thermometer edges down toward zero—centigrade. On clear, but frigid winter days they are seen stamping their feet in a vain effort to stay warm, and tales of frozen fingers and benumbed toes make the rounds in the immigrant community. For Brazilians used to their land's tropical and semi-tropical climes, such conditions are particularly onerous, but they have no choice but to put up with them because they receive no pay if they stay indoors. Then, there are the very long hours. Ten hour days are typical for book sellers who begin at 8:00 or 9:00 AM and work until 6:00 or 7:00. Those selling food—hotdogs, soft pretzels, cold drinks, sugared peanuts—have somewhat shorter hours since food sales only pick up at mid-day.

Street vendors' long hours spent at the mercy of the elements are not rewarded by their earnings. Since the income from street sales varies widely with the weather and the season, it is more irregular and more uncertain than the income from any other job that Brazilian immigrants hold. Vendors say that under icy wintry conditions pedestrians hurry by not bothering to stop for a hotdog or a pretzel or to leaf through their displays of large "coffee table" books. Food sales pick up as temperatures moderate and are best on balmy spring and summer days. Book sales take off in November and December as the holidays approach.

Even in the best of times the income from these activities is not very attractive to Brazilian immigrants trying to earn as much money in as little time as possible. For book sellers, earnings usually range from $30 to $50 a day, although they can be quite a bit more during the frenzied pre-Christmas shopping season. Still, it is difficult to generalize about average income because it literally changes with the weather. For example, in a week of six sunny days, a food vendor can earn $300, but with three days of rain, income can be halved to $150. Thus, street vending has all the disadvantages of the low-wage, service jobs open to immigrants, especially those new to this country. Just imagine a job in which, day after day, you put in long hours standing on a street corner in all kinds of weather not knowing how much money you were going to earn for all your effort! It is little wonder, then, that at the first opportunity Brazilian immigrants give up their jobs on the streets for something a little better paying and more secure, usually indoors.

Building New York

An article on Brazilian immigrants in *Veja*, a Brazilian newsmagazine similar to *Time*, reported that immigrants from Governador Valadares were sometimes hired in teams by labor contractors in the United States. One man from the town, for example, headed a work crew of about fifteen of his fellow citizens who painted bridges in New Jersey. "This is a very closed market," he is quoted as saying. "The only way to get these positions is through labor contractors." Although now back home in Brazil, he still receives calls from American labor contractors seeking workers (Corrêa 1994:74).

Brazilian immigrants who work in construction in New York City are far less organized than their compatriots from Governador Valadares, that famed exporter of *brazucas* (Portuguese slang for Brazilians living in the United States), nor do they paint bridges. Brazilians in the city's construction industry do a variety of unskilled jobs involved in home and office painting and renovation. Some also work in demolition, paving, cement mixing, brick making, and hauling building materials. In New York City about as many Brazilian men work in construction as drive radio call cars and in New York's suburbs, construction and renovation jobs are probably the single most important source of male employment. Brazilians are but one of many newcomers to New York who work in construction where there is a strong immigrant presence in those parts of the building industry that are unlicensed and not unionized (Freedman 1983).

Neither Brazilians nor other recent immigrants work in the skilled building trades—as masons, electricians, carpenters and so on. Without connections, skilled union jobs are difficult to come by even for American citizens, and Brazilian immigrants rarely have the training to be employed in them anyway. Recall that most Brazilian immigrants had white collar or professional jobs in Brazil and that from the Brazilian perspective, manual labor, even skilled manual labor, signifies humble status.

Most of the construction jobs available to undocumented immigrants are short-term and layoffs and job changes are frequent. Another disadvantage of this work is the seasonality of many jobs in the industry. Construction in New York involving work outdoors usually ceases from about mid-December to mid-March and Brazilians scramble to find other temporary jobs. A few lucky Brazilians whose green cards permit them to come and go from the United States as they please, simply head south to summer in Brazil, where the seasons are the reverse of those in the United States.

Brazilian Specialties

If you were asked what are "typical jobs" for immigrants new to the United States, you might mention some of those already named—dish washing and busing tables, housekeeping and child care, perhaps driving a cab. But aside from this familiar terrain, Brazilian immigrants in New York City also dominate two other job niches that certainly would not come to mind: shoe shining and gogo dancing. While the number of Brazilian immigrants who shine shoes or dance in bars is relatively small, in Brazil's mass media and the nation's psyche shoe shining and gogo dancing loom large as the archetypical work of their immigrant compatriots in the United States. That shoeshine "boys" and gogo "girls" represent immigrant employment in Brazilian discourse rests not on their numbers but on their dominance in these two small corners of the city's labor market. Brazilian men have a near monopoly—perhaps 90 or 95 percent—of the shoeshining jobs in the shoe repair shops and shoe shine stands that dot Manhattan, and Brazilian women reign supreme as gogo dancers, at one time holding up to 80 percent of such jobs in bars in New York City and throughout the metropolitan area.

As with most jobs that Brazilian immigrants hold, figures are illusive. What is certain is that shoe shining employs only a small fraction of Brazilians compared, for example, to restaurant work. While many Brazilian men work as shoeshiners,[5] far more wash dishes and bus tables. It also stands to reason that the demand for gogo dancers is minuscule compared to the job market for live-in housekeepers, maids and nannies, so that far fewer Brazilian women earn their living as dancers than as domestic servants.

How did Brazilians come to dominate these two small domains in the city's sprawling labor market? Once again, Governador Valadares takes center stage. The roots of Brazilian shoeshiners date back to the mid-1960s when, through a migratory path that remains unclear, two brothers from that city found jobs as shoeshiners in midtown Manhattan. Word filtered back of the money to be made and by the end of the decade a small contingent of Brazilians were shining shoes in the vicinity of Grand Central Station. Their numbers slowly increased as networks of friends and relatives found shoeshine jobs for new arrivals in the city, and by the early 1980s this job sector—once the domain of African Americans—was monopolized by Brazilians.

The route by which Brazilian immigrants came to dominate New York's gogo dancing jobs follows the same improbable path. Women from Governador Valadares began arriving in New York in the late 1960s or early 1970s, perhaps at the behest of male shoeshining relatives. At first the women were employed as domestic servants at modest salaries, but soon one or more found jobs dancing in bars—work that paid three times what they had been making as housecleaners. Word of these earnings made its way back to Brazil and other would-be dancers arrived. The flow of immigrant gogos continued through the 1980s then lured by the prospect of earning $400 or $500 a week. Some dancers fanned out of the city and found work at bars in the New York suburbs and in New Jersey.

It is impossible to say how many Brazilian women are employed as gogo dancers in bars and nightclubs in the region. One Brazilian—a pioneer gogo dancer herself back in the 1970s—estimated that there are between 2,000 and 3,000 gogo dancers throughout the greater New York metropolitan area and that until

---

5. I had once thought that shoeshining was a male monopoly, but after completing my research I encountered two Brazilian women shining shoes in a midtown Manhattan shoe repair shop.

around 1990, some 70 to 80 percent were Brazilian. Since then Russian immigrant women have made major inroads into the profession.

But whatever the actual number, gogo dancing is still the most lucrative career track available to Brazilian immigrant women. In what other job can new immigrants, especially those without work papers, earn up to $300 a night? The earnings of gogo dancers vary by bar, by the generosity of their clientele and by the number of days and hours they are willing to work. Since income is from both wages and tips, it fluctuates widely although most dancers average $150 to $200 a night.

Income from that other Brazilian forte, shining shoes, is not nearly so high as it is from gogo dancing, but it is still appealing to people used to Brazilian pay scales. Most of what shoeshiners earn comes from tips since the shoeshine stands and shoe repair shops that employ them either pay nothing at all or a nominal $10 to $15 a day. Because of this wage structure, income from this job, like that of so many others open to undocumented immigrants, swings wildly. It varies with the time of year and the weather— when it rains or snows, customers disappear. A shoeshiner's income ultimately depends on how many regular customers he has and how generous they are with their tips. On a busy day a man with many steady customers working in a well located shop can earn $70 or $80, although most average around $50 a day or $250 a week, still very good pay by Brazilian standards. In both gogo dancing and shoeshining, wages are paid in cash, as are tips, so that the income from them is "off-the-books." Thus, the figures cited refer to net income.

Aside from Brazilians who ply their trade at the city's shoe repair shops and shoeshine stands, some are employed as independent shoeshiners who cater to businessmen with offices in Manhattan skyscrapers. Many immigrants prefer this work to shining shoes in stores or kiosks because the independent gets to keep not only his tips, but the money the customer pays for the shoeshine as well. Moreover, working hours can be shorter and more flexible than those at a street level shop, and independents also delight in the fact that they are their own bosses and can work the days and hours that they wish.

Both shoeshiners and gogo dancers work long hours for their pay. A shoeshiner's day starts at 7:00 to 7:30 AM and does not end until the last customer leaves with a shine on his shoes around

6:00 in the evening. Gogo dancers usually come to work at 8:00 or 9:00 PM and stay until 3:00 or 4:00 AM. Of course, the women are not dancing all this time. A dancer will do a set of twenty or thirty minutes, usually accompanied by one or two other dancers. Then she will change clothes and may sit at the bar drinking or chatting with patrons while other dancers perform the next set. She then changes back into her costume and dances again. A shift lasts anywhere from five to eight hours, but gogo dancers intent on earning money quickly can work double shifts since some bars open around noon and have continuous performances until closing time in the wee small hours of the morning.

All of this appears straightforward enough but gogo dancing, more than any other job held by Brazilian immigrants, is a very problematic calling. Evidence for this comes from the fact that in conversations with me, Brazilian men were no more reluctant to discuss shining shoes than washing dishes or doing other menial jobs, while Brazilian women employed as gogo dancers were loath to talk about their work. The difficulty I had interviewing these women strongly suggests that most of them do not view gogo dancing as just another job. And, if they feel constrained talking about their work with a nosy American researcher, they are even more evasive with their friends and relatives in Brazil, often telling them that the good money they earn comes from long hours spent "cleaning apartments" or "baby sitting."

Gogo dancers work in an all-male environment. Bar patrons usually are all men and the only women in the bars are the dancers themselves and perhaps a barmaid. The bars in which dancers work vary by neighborhood. There are "sleazy" bars and "upscale" bars; the two are distinguished by their location, their clientele and their general ambience. The jurisdiction in which a bar is located also affects working conditions. Striptease, for example, is legal in New York but not in New Jersey. In that state women may not dance topless—instead, they wear tiny string bikinis. And bar owners cannot insist that dancers mingle with customers after the show. New York puts fewer legal restrictions on performers and topless dancing is standard. Dancers who work in gogo bars in Manhattan are generally expected to encourage patrons to buy drinks and in some establishments they get a percentage of each drink sold.

Gogo dancers' extreme reluctance to discuss their employment is understandable given the seaminess of their work and its dark aura of degradation. Dancers are often subject to harassment. Most complain about being on-going targets of sexual advances and lewd remarks. They are pawed by drunken patrons and constantly fend off unwanted proposals from customers who lie in wait for them outside the bars when they get off work. Both patrons and male bar employees hound them for dates, viewing gogo dancers as fair game by virtue of their occupation. These attitudes and actions reflect the stereotype that gogo dancers are nothing but prostitutes in disguise and that many abuse drugs as well. Most Brazilian dancers and their friends vigorously deny these allegations, insisting that few, if any, of their compatriots engage in such behavior. But whatever the case may be—and data on illicit activities are obviously difficult to come by—the image persists and it is the basis for gogo dancers' profound unease when questioned about their profession.

Going It Alone

"The Brazilian community is mostly one of employees not employers," I was told soon after I began my field research in New York City. And, for the most part, this turned out to be true. Brazilian immigrants have no entrepreneurial niche like that of the Korean green grocer, the Indian newstand dealer, the Greek street vendor or the Mexican flower seller. Most Brazilian immigrants see themselves as sojourners not permanent settlers in the city, making them more likely to "take the money and run," as one Brazilian put it, than to invest in a future in the United States.

Although they are the exception not the rule, there are Brazilian immigrants who have started businesses in New York, some of which have become quite successful. Little Brazil, the block-long street in midtown Manhattan that is the commercial heart of the Brazilian community, has its fair share of immigrant entrepreneurs, albeit ones who arrived in the city two and three decades ago. These oldtimers own a variety of businesses that cater to Brazilian tourists and immigrants alike—restaurants, travel and remittance agencies, stores selling Brazilian products and others featuring small electronic goods primarily aimed at the tourist market.

More modest Brazilian-owned businesses that cater exclusively to the immigrant community are located in Astoria, Queens, the city's primary Brazilian residential neighborhood. Here newstands, grocery stores, luncheonettes and snack bars carry all manner of items from back home—Brazilian newspapers and magazines, compact discs, videos of Brazilian TV shows and sports events, Brazilian brands of beer and soft drinks, *farinha de mandioca* (manioc flour) which is a staple of the Brazilian diet, and even the tiny Brazilian-made string bikinis called "dental floss" (*fio dental*) in Portuguese. There are also beauty salons with a largely Brazilian clientele, travel agencies featuring charter flights to Rio de Janeiro and São Paulo, and remittance agencies that guarantee next day delivery of immigrants' hard earned dollars to waiting relatives back in Brazil.

Astoria is also home base to several Brazilian-owned radio call car companies, one of the city's few enterprises started by Brazilian immigrants that do not have an exclusively Brazilian clientele. The companies' immigrant founders themselves worked as call car drivers and then set up dispatcher services used by other drivers. Stretch limousines—upscale variants of radio call cars—are also available for hire from two thriving enterprises, both founded by Brazilian immigrants.

Then there are the Brazilians who have shunned pedestrian enterprises aimed at their fellow ethnics, preferring instead to hitch their entrepreneurial stars to the growing popularity of things Brazilian. In recent years New York has been awash with Brazilian performers and musicians. Hardly a week goes by when some well-known Brazilian talent is not performing at Lincoln Center, Carnegie Hall or some less famous venue. Free concerts of Brazilian music in Central Park draw not only Brazilian natives, but scores of American aficionados as well. About a dozen restaurants and nightclubs in Manhattan have responded to this vogue by featuring Brazilian food and music. Two or three expatriate bands travel the New York nightclub circuit playing Brazilian *samba, bossa nova* and *forró,* and companies of Brazilian singers, dancers and musicians have been formed to capitalize on the Brazilian music craze. A nearly all-Brazilian cast of twenty-five dancers and musicians sporting elaborate Carmen Miranda-like costumes performs four or five shows a month at private parties, bar mitzvahs, nightclubs and carnival balls around the New York metropolitan area.

While acknowledging the entrepreneurs of Little Brazil and Astoria, many of the city's long-time Brazilian residents lament the general lack of business acumen among their newly arrived

When Brazilians eat dinner out they often go to restaurants that feature the food of their homeland, such as this one on Little Brazil Street.

compatriots. "Why is it that Koreans, Indians and Chinese all have booming businesses, while Brazilians have nothing?" they ask with evident chagrin, apparently unaware of several other small scale ventures started by fellow Brazilians. There is, for example, the family that regularly sells Brazilian food, beer and soft drinks at the city's street fairs and the dozen or so Brazilian women who do catering from their apartments in Queens. These and other mundane Brazilian-owned enterprises—a delivery service, an auto body shop, an electronics repair shop, a paving company, a towing service, a painting company—escape the notice of most Brazilian residents. Since these small businesses encompass a multiplicity of money-making ventures, they are easily overlooked.

This, then, is a sketch of the low-wage service sector in which most Brazilians and so many other new immigrants find themselves. We can now understand why the labor of new immigrants, whether documented or not, is sought after by employers in this segment of the American economy. Immigrants are valued not only because of the relatively low cost of their labor, but because of the temporary nature of their migration. At least at first, most immigrants view their stay in the United States as short-lived. And so, however much they may deny it, Brazilians and other international migrants are sought by American employers. As an abundant source of inexpensive but often well educated labor, they are an employer's dream: workers who are willing, even eager, to take a variety of jobs that otherwise might go unfilled.

But taking menial jobs carries a price. Brazilian immigrants in New York do work that would be considered "way beneath" them back home. How do they deal with this social descent? And how do they adjust to being new immigrants in the maelstrom of one of the world's greatest cities? These are the subjects of the next chapter.

4

Immigrant Life in Gotham City

The life of Brazilians, like that of so many other immigrants new to New York City, is fraught with challenges and travails. Brazilian immigrants not only have to come to terms with working at low status, menial jobs that would be unthinkable back home, they also have to weather the long hours of drudgery that the jobs often entail. They have to contend with a dizzying cacophony of English—a language few newcomers speak with any fluency—as they move around an alien metropolis with its baffling transportation hubs, frenzied street life and daunting pace. They have to deal with the high cost of living in a city that bills itself "the capital of the world" as they find a place to live and forge a modest existence, all the while trying to save as much money as possible for the return home. As if all this were not enough, many immigrants also worry about their undocumented status, constantly looking over their shoulders for the fearsome spectre of *Tia Mimi* (Aunt Mimi), Portuguese slang for the United States Immigration and Naturalization Service. And perhaps hardest of all, these experiences are lived under the poignant shadow of *saudades,* "the memories which touch a soul," the aching longing for home, for family and friends, for the familiar (Feldman-Bianco 1992:45).

The Fall from Grace

One of the first harsh facts of New York life that recent arrivals from Brazil have to face is the profound loss of status that accompanies their employment. Given their middle class roots and the negative eye with which Brazilians from this social stratum view manual labor, it is little wonder that they suffer from their downward social track, finding it one of their most difficult crosses to bear as immigrants.

Take domestic service as an example. In Brazil, class differences are often displayed in manner and attitude. Domestic servants, who are near the bottom of the nation's social scale, are expected to be submissive in exchanges with their employers. This dance of deference requires that servants stand passively in their employer's presence and generally not speak until spoken to. They address their *patrões* (bosses) with heads slightly bowed and eyes lowered, always using the respectful terms *o senhor* and *a senhora* when talking to them, the male and female forms of "you" in Portuguese. Servants, in turn, are called *você* by their employers, the more familiar form of "you" used in addressing children and between close friends and relatives.

Just imagine what such work means to a middle-class Brazilian in New York who suddenly finds herself transformed into a domestic servant. Back home it is she who would be the employer since nearly all middle-class families in Brazil have household help. Time and again during the course of my research I encountered just such women—lawyers, social workers, engineers, psychologists and teachers—working as live-in housekeepers, day maids and baby sitters. The disdainful treatment of domestic workers in Brazil, the menial nature of their jobs, and the profound inequality inherent in the employer-servant dyad all contribute to making domestic service highly problematic for Brazilian immigrants. For the middle class Brazilian woman working as a domestic, the breach between her social background and her current occupation makes for a crash course in downward mobility.

Brazilian women cope with their degraded status in various ways. Some use humor. Women joke about how incompetent they are at housework; after all, they had servants to do it in Brazil. Others try to compartmentalize their life and work by putting themselves in a sort of disassociative state when they are scrubbing floors or doing laundry. Still others take great pains to conceal the nature of their jobs from family members in Brazil. But the conviction that such work is short-term is what gets most of them through the day. Because a majority of Brazilians, at least initially, come to the United States as sojourners not as settlers, they are more easily reconciled to their menial jobs and the accompanying loss of status that they bring; they view both the jobs and their social descent as temporary.

Domestic service is not the only occupation held by Brazilian immigrants that means a sharp decline in rank. Restaurant employment also impairs social standing and causes similar anxiety among male immigrants. In Brazil, work as a waiter or busboy would be out of the question for anyone with much more than a primary school education, but in New York I met Brazilians with professional degrees who were busing tables and washing dishes. And, despite what can be excellent pay in upscale Manhattan restaurants, in Brazil such jobs have the dual taints of low wages and low status, and most Brazilian immigrants continue to see them in the same light albeit in a new setting.

STRANGERS IN A STRANGE LAND

Aside from what they must endure at work, Brazilian immigrants —like all new immigrants—are subject to a daily barrage of shocks to their sense of the familiar. The lack of proficiency in English does not make things any easier. Sixty percent of the Brazilians in my study rated their English as "fair to poor," while only 13 percent said it was "excellent or fluent." Just imagine being in their position; living amid the meaningless swirl of an unknown language in a foreign culture. "People who don't speak English suffer a lot in New York," one Brazilian told me. "To come here without speaking English is suicide," another said. Some blamed the solitude that many immigrants feel in the United States on their lack of fluency in English; without it they cannot fully participate in the bustling life that surrounds them.

The inability to speak English well and the sense of isolation and loneliness that that entails enhances feelings of alienation especially among immigrants without relatives in New York. To live apart from one's family is always viewed as a hardship by Brazilians regardless of the reasons for the separation. When I was a graduate student and spent six weeks doing research on a sugar estate in Bahia, Brazilians continually asked me how I could "bear to be so far away from my family for so long."

In this respect the contrast between life in Brazil and life in the United States is particularly striking. Aside from their immediate families, people in Brazil typically see other relatives—aunts, uncles, cousins, grandparents, married siblings—on a regular, even a daily basis. Relatives tend to live near each other, and in large cities family members often have apartments in the same building (Miller 1979). Moreover, in Brazil—which lacks a tradition of "going away to college" or "going out on one's own"—adult children do not leave home until they marry. That many Americans go off to college in their late teens and early twenties or leave their parents to live alone or move in with friends is viewed as both odd and lamentable by Brazilian immigrants. "Why," they ask, "would anyone *want* to live apart from their family?"

Also, recall that another American trait that Brazilians find strange is the desire for privacy. Social life in Brazil usually revolves around family members who think nothing of dropping in on each other unannounced. But, as Brazilian immigrants soon learn, one does not do that in the United States; the doors of people's houses are not open to friends and relatives like they are in Brazil. As one immigrant advises her newly arrived compatriots, "Americans value their privacy and you should never just show up at an American's home without making a date first."

Some culture shocks to an immigrant's sense of the familiar are more abstract. A common Brazilian complaint about New York involves its quality of life—its frenetic pace, the incivility of its salespeople and bus drivers, the anonymous crowds of subway riders and the throngs of pedestrians jostling for space on cramped Manhattan sidewalks. Brazilians cite the avoidance of eye contact between strangers on the street, a subway train or bus as odd or foreign or simply "unBrazilian." This lack of engagement, in turn, is linked to a more encompassing complaint about the United States. The "American personality" is "cold," I was told, or at least "more restrained" compared to the "Brazilian personality." It lacks *calor humano,* an indefinable blend of human warmth and empathy.

But Brazilians also have high praise for certain aspects of American life and institutions, particularly in comparison with their counterparts back home. Brazilian immigrants in Boston, for example, put a positive spin on the respectful and "egalitarian" treatment they had received from merchants and local authorities in certain cities despite their poor English and the questionable legal status of some. Many immigrants are impressed by what they perceive as the efficiency of social welfare and law enforcement in the United States. They also feel less threatened by violence than they do in Brazil and have more confidence in the local police.[1] Then, too, they are favorably impressed by the relatively relaxed, easy going relationship between employers and employees in the United States; it is "respectful" and "more professional" than in Brazil, especially in the status minefield of domestic service (Martes 1996). These sorts of positive, even idealized views of the host country are common among immigrants, particularly new arrivals (Suárez-Orozco and Suárez-Orozco 1995).

Other immigrants value the laissez-faire, "do your own thing" attitude of New Yorkers. "You can wear what you like here and no one bothers you or criticizes you or even *looks* at you," a woman from Rio de Janeiro told me. And poor dress does not mean poor treatment, as it so often does in Brazil, where a man in work clothes or a woman in a housedress and flip flops will be left cooling their heels for hours in a doctor's waiting room or at a bank or government office, while a man in a suit and tie or an elegantly dressed woman will be immediately ushered in.

Of course, the opportunity to earn what Brazilian immigrants consider "good money" is often cited as a prime feature of American life. They also admire the apparent health of the United States economy which, unlike the one they were used to back home, has not been wracked by rampant inflation. To immigrants, a stable economy means the ability to save and plan for the future, a near impossibility during Brazil's long inflation nightmare. Then, too, some Brazilians are very taken with American buying power. To Brazilians the fact that an "ordinary" middle class citizen—that is, one who is not rich—can simply go out and buy a stereo or a color television set or a VCR, without pay-

---

1. In recent years police in some Brazilian cities, like Rio de Janeiro, have been charged with rampant corruption and have been accused of murdering street children for pay.

ing for it on time with hefty interest charges or planning for it months in advance, is enticing indeed.

There are also the singular attractions of living in "the capital of the world" with its kaleidoscope of peoples and cultures, pulsing street life, glittering skyline and "canyons of steel." Brazilian immigrants also recounted the subtle appeals of life in New York City: the enchantment of a first snowfall, the experience of autumn in Central Park, a long dreamed of visit to the top of the Empire State Building, an evening bus ride down the bright neon wall of Broadway to Times Square. Some Brazilians were so taken with the delights of New York City that they sounded more like tourists on holiday than immigrants struggling to earn money in menial jobs. One immigrant, a widow from Rio de Janeiro, declared that she had "returned to life in New York." And another Brazilian pointed out that, while many of her compatriots go back to Brazil with the intention of staying, some turn right around and fly back to the United States because "New York is like a vice, people get addicted. They just keep coming back for more."

IN PURSUIT OF VERDINHAS

Brazilian immigrants in New York call U.S. dollars *verdinhas*, "little green things." Many say that earning and saving them are among the most difficult problems they face as immigrants because life in this country is so costly. The Brazilian media's image of the United States notwithstanding, immigrants soon learn that *verdinhas* do not grow on trees. Brazilians fault themselves and their compatriots for the mirage of the "easy buck," for their grand delusions about what a dollar buys and what it takes to earn. One immigrant likened Brazilians who come to New York to the poverty stricken migrants of Brazil's northeast who travel south to São Paulo on *pão de araras* ("parrot's perches," crowded open air trucks) in search of jobs and a better life. Both migrant streams involve similar "deceptive dreams of riches," he said.

Brazilian immigrants often spoke of how they were deluded about the material realities of life in the United States. They talked of how foolish they were to believe that after working for two or three years in this country they could return home with $40,000 or $50,000 in savings. They recounted their naive faith in the absurd notion that someone could actually live in New York City on a minimum wage of $4.25 or $5.15 an hour, a figure that initially sounds like a lot of money to people from a country like Brazil where the minimum wage is just over $100 *a month*. Many immigrants were also taken aback by the high cost of housing in the city, and decried the steep rents they had to pay for even spartan dwellings.

In truth, there are probably fewer misconceptions about the earning power of new immigrants in the United States than the discourse of some Brazilians would suggest. I met very few immigrants who actually expected to return to Brazil, their pockets bulging with *verdinhas*. Most were more realistic about their likely savings; $10,000 or $20,000 over two to three years were the most common figures I heard. Moreover, immigrants' plans for the money were equally modest: to make a downpayment on a piece of property in Brazil—a house, a condominium, some land or a small business. For a few the goal was more immediate; to earn enough to send remittances to their families back home. However, it is indeed true that most immigrants were genuinely stunned by the high cost of living in New York City and we already know their responses to this reality: sharing living quarters and utilities, renting rooms to compatriots, spending the bare minimum on furnishings and clothing, and generally living as frugally as possible—at least during their first months in the city.

Brazilian immigrants in New York also undergo a quick reality check when they discover just how hard they have to work to achieve their goals. Given their relatively low wages, the expense of living in a world capital like New York and their intention of saving money for the return home, Brazilians have to labor very long hours, indeed, often working at two jobs. Once again, words like "illusion" are used in reference to what making "good money" entails in a city like New York. Brazilians have "no real understanding of what it is like to work in the United States," I was told, because former migrants returning to Brazil "brag about how much money they earned. They make it sound so easy." As a result, the real life experience of twelve or thirteen hour days comes as a shock, said one immigrant, contrasting this with the eight hour day typical of middle-class jobs in Brazil. "So of course, they suffer," he concluded.

ON THE LOOKOUT

Were they aware of it, one piece of information that might brighten the lives of undocumented Brazilians and other "out of status" (undocumented) immigrants in New York City is that the U.S. Immigration and Naturalization Service (INS) virtually ignores visa overstayers. The INS has no specific program to locate and deport the estimated 150,000 "visitors" who overstay their tourist and student visas to the United States each year and the agency has devoted very few resources to this sector of the undocumented population. In New York, for example, the task of investigating work places for undocumented immigrants falls to fifteen INS agents in fourteen counties with a combined population of more than 12 million people! The absence of INS policy is evident from the agency's own statistics; in 1994, only 500 of the close to 40,000 deportees from the United States were visa overstayers. Then, too, the INS tends to raid sweatshops that employ undocumented Mexicans and Chinese, rather than businesses—like restaurants—that employ immigrants from other nations (Irish, Poles, Brazilians, Canadians) who are undocumented because they overstay their visas. Finally, undocumented immigrants in New York City have even less to fear than those in some other parts of the country because since 1986 a city executive order has been in force which bans city agencies from notifying the INS about undocumented immigrants, if such notification would prevent them from enrolling their children in school, reporting a crime or seeking medical aid[2] (Dunn 1995; U.S. Immigration and Naturalization Service 1996; Hunt 1996; Schmitt 1996).

But these facts are unknown to most undocumented immigrants, including Brazilians, so the fear of apprehension and deportation by INS agents is very real. Indeed, there are occasional raids on sweatshops or other businesses employing large numbers of undocumented workers. For example, a raid on an office cleaning business in Newark rounded up sixty undocumented

---

2. As this book goes to press, New York City is suing the U.S. government to prevent enforcement of a provision in the new federal welfare law that would allow city employees to report undocumented immigrants who seek services like medical care, police protection or public education to the immigration authorities (Firestone 1996).

workers from Brazil and Portugal (*Brazilian Voice* 1995). Another case in point is a shoeshine shop near Grand Central Station. Two years after completing my original research on Brazilian immigrants in New York City, I returned to the shop—long an employer of undocumented Brazilians—that I had visited many times before. Unprompted, the owner told me that he "had had to fire at least forty shoeshiners" when he "suddenly" found out he was employing "illegal aliens" who lacked green cards. He claimed that the INS had begun enforcing the law and that he is "in court" as a result. He now demands to see a green card or a social security card or he will not hire the person because "its just not worth it." But, then he offered a caveat: "Since Americans won't do this work," he told me, he will still hire someone without papers, "if the shop is very busy."

The nation's burgeoning anti-immigrant sentiment also has heightened distrust among those without papers. My own experience is illustrative. I noted a marked change in tone when I revisited several upscale Manhattan restaurants in which I had previously interviewed Brazilian employees. Where I had once been greeted with friendly curiosity as a Portuguese-speaking American and with an apparent eagerness to engage in conversation, Brazilian employees now were very reluctant to talk to me. Although I again spoke Portuguese and only asked innocuous questions like: "Where do you come from in Brazil?" many appeared suspicious of my interest in them and cut short our conversation. Surely this change in behavior must have had something to do with the heated polemics that now envelope the hot button issue of "illegal aliens."

Even before the recent attention to undocumented immigration, however, fear of *Tia Mimi* the Portuguese slang term for United States immigration authorities, affected the lives of many Brazilian immigrants in New York City. Anxiety about *Tia Mimi* is present almost from the moment that many would-be immigrants get off the plane at Kennedy Airport and pass through immigration inspection where their motives for visiting this country may be questioned.

This anxiety continues to shadow Brazilian immigrants as they go about their lives in the city. Under the misconception that to do so would put them at risk, some undocumented Brazilians are reluctant to provide their local addresses when filling out forms of any kind—applications to open a bank account or to apply for a job, forms to send remittances to Brazil or to get a driver's license. For the same reason, some Brazilians avoid contact with the Brazilian Consulate erroneously assuming that consular personnel are obligated to turn undocumented immigrants over to the American authorities. Then, too, afraid to call attention to themselves, many are hesitant to report crimes against them to the New York police. Even living arrangements are colored by fear. One Brazilian suggested to me that his compatriots reside together in crowded apartments not just to save money but for security; they feel there is safety in numbers.

The apprehension surrounding their undocumented status, along with the burning desire to visit relatives and friends in Brazil—something immigrants without papers cannot easily do because they run the risk of not being allowed back into the United States—leads some Brazilians to spend thousands of dollars in the often fruitless quest for a green card. Unscrupulous lawyers are more than willing to take advantage of these fears. Self-styled "immigration counselors" prey on undocumented Brazilians and other immigrants and for a fee of $2,500 to $3,000 "guarantee" to get them green cards through a non-existent "amnesty program" (Apsan 1995).

A somewhat more certain path to legalization is through marriage to an American citizen. While many such marriages are based on love and companionship, a significant but unknown number involve the pursuit of something else: a green card. These so-called green card marriages, in which an immigrant marries for the sole purpose of obtaining a green card, most commonly involve a Brazilian marrying an American citizen of Hispanic origin, often a Puerto Rican. These arrangements are both costly and time consuming. The would-be American spouse receives anywhere from $5000 to $10,000 and the process takes two or three years. During this time the couple must submit to a series of interviews with immigration officers and demonstrate that they have filed joint tax returns. Then, with green card in hand, and after paying an additional hefty sum to an attorney, divorce papers are filed and the marriage is dissolved.

Parenthetically, in New York City about 1200 people a month petition the U.S. Immigration Service for legal residency based on their marriage to American citizens. One INS agent compared the separate interviews of spouses to TV's "Newlywed Game" because the couple are questioned about the intimate details of their lives to determine if they actually live together. In the end, about 16 percent of those interviewed are denied green cards because the INS believes the marriages to be fraudulent (Sontag 1994).

TIES THAT DO NOT BIND

The uneasy suspicion of some in New York's Brazilian immigrant community that INS agents lurk around every corner is tied to the premise that there are informers in their midst. I was told that the threat of "don't do that to me or I'll call Tia Mimi" was not an idle one and that more than a few Brazilians turned in their compatriots for monetary gain. The INS purportedly pays $500 for useful tips on the whereabouts of undocumented workers. Still, I was unable to document a single case of Brazilians informing on one another to the INS and believe, in fact, that this rarely occurs.

Why, then, the prevailing notion that Brazilians betray each other to the authorities? This is but one ingredient in the wide ranging discourse among Brazilian immigrants about rampant "bad" behavior among their fellow ethnics in New York City. From my first day of field work, Brazilians bombarded me with an array of complaints about their compatriots. Again and again, I was told Brazilians "only think of themselves," "don't help each other," "cheat on each other" and "don't want other Brazilians to get ahead." Some immigrants declared that they had few or no Brazilian friends and that when they heard people speaking Portuguese they crossed the street to avoid them because they "don't want anything to do with Brazilians."

One recurrent theme in this discourse is that, in New York, Brazilians are transformed into their evil twins. They go from being generous, caring individuals to selfish, self-centered louts. "It's unfortunate that people become so cold and egotistical here," a Brazilian immigrant told me. Interestingly, immigrants themselves blame neither the New York environment nor American institutions for this purported transformation. Rather, it is their own pursuit of the almighty dollar that is held responsible. "Immigrants begin to think only about money when they come here," another Brazilian said. "They live by a different ethic in the

United States than they do in Brazil." Moreover, these complaints are not limited to Brazilian immigrants in New York City. In Miami, another major center of Brazilian immigration, one new arrival is quoted as saying, "It's not like it was in Brazil. Here everyone is for himself" (Neto and Bernardes 1996:56).

Examples of "bad" behavior were legion. I was told tales of Brazilians charging each other for carrying money back to their families in Brazil or for doing each other even the most minor favor. One immigrant recounted with disgust how another Brazilian—whom she had considered a friend—charged her a week's wages for finding her a job as a live-in housekeeper. Even though she detested the job and left after a week or two, her "friend" refused to return the finder's fee. Martes (1995b) also reports the practice of selling cleaning jobs among Brazilian immigrants in Boston. There too, even if the job does not work out and the buyer is fired, the money is not returned. Other stories of misbehavior involved "job stealing." Said one immigrant: when Brazilians see new compatriots arrive in New York, their first thought is: "Have they come to grab my job?"

While these allegations of boorish behavior are probably exaggerated, some softening of ethical standards does, in fact, occur. This is not due to any special failing of Brazilians as a national cohort, but rather to the immigrant experience itself. Research suggests Brazilians are not the only immigrants decrying the change in their compatriots' behavior after they arrive in the United States. Immigrants from El Salvador living on New York's Long Island, for example, were dismayed that "the common courtesies and reciprocities of their home country lives had not migrated to the United States with them." While Salvadorans had expected to be exploited by Americans, "they did not come prepared to be taken advantage of by their own coethnic peers" (Mahler 1995:32, 102). And in a community of Russian-Jewish immigrants in California, "feelings of distrust and individualism are pervasive" causing many émigrés to distance themselves from their compatriots (Gold 1995:90). Political scientist Michael J. Piore's stark portrait of the material motives that fuel the lives of most new immigrants helps explain these bitter complaints. Immigrants, he writes, "are people divorced from a social setting, operating outside the constraints and inhibitions that it imposes, working totally and exclusively for money" (Piore 1979:55). Obviously such single-minded determination is detrimental both to inter-personal relations and to community-building.

Indeed, the Brazilian critique was not limited to individuals; it extended to Brazilians collectively and to local Brazilian institutions as well. "Brazilians are the most disunited ethnic group in the city," I was told. This declaration was repeated again and again by Brazilians who lamented the fact that, unlike many other immigrant groups in New York, Brazilians failed to cooperate with each other and to organize on their own behalf. A feeble community *esprit de corps* was blamed for the lack of Brazilian social clubs, community groups and mutual aid societies, and, once again, these complaints are not heard exclusively from Brazilians in New York. In Miami, much to the chagrin of many Brazilians living there, a community network of aid that they thought would provide new immigrants with support, simply does not exist (Neto and Bernardes 1996).

Brazilian immigrants offered contending explanations for this dearth of unity and collective vitality. One woman, a long-time New York resident, blamed the city's burgeoning Brazilian population. When she first arrived far fewer Brazilians were living there and since "everyone knew everyone else" this meant a greater sense of community solidarity. Another Brazilian cited the distrust that pervades any group with a large contingent of undocumented individuals. Fear of informers prevents an easygoing sociality with compatriots who are not close friends and relatives. Still other immigrants cited personalistic factors: the absence of dynamic, high-minded community leaders to unify Brazilians and promote their common interests.

Several Brazilians noted that in New York they not only lack a social community but a physical community as well, a distinctly Brazilian neighborhood to call their own. Even the block dubbed "Little Brazil" in Manhattan is not entirely theirs.[3] It has a heterogeneous mix of enterprises with Japanese, Argentine, Korean and Italian restaurants as well as many businesses of no obvious nationality. And in Astoria, Queens, their main residential neighborhood in the city, the Brazilian presence is also muted. A few

---

3. In June, 1996 New York City Mayor Rudolph Giuliani signed legislation officially naming West 46th Street in Manhattan "Little Brazil Street."

scattered stores selling Brazilian magazines, videos and other products, a take-out restaurant and a handful of other Brazilian-owned businesses are lost in a multi-ethnic sea.

Perhaps tied to the lack of a physical community is the underwhelming scale of Brazilian enterprises in New York City, that is, businesses that could provide newly arrived immigrants with jobs. Brazilians have no equivalent of the Korean green grocery or the Indian newsstand, no distinct occupational niche with which they are identified. And with no ready source of employment within their own community, there is no economic basis for ethnic solidarity (Bonacich and Modell 1980). "Quite the contrary," said one immigrant, "The few Brazilians who do own businesses not only are no help to new immigrants, they exploit them, pay them less and make them work longer hours." Nor do established Brazilian enterprises like the New York branches of Brazilian banks, airlines and major companies provide support for individuals or institutions within the immigrant community.

Brazilian tradition also helps explain the paucity of social cohesion and local ethnic structures in New York. Brazil has a less developed tradition of membership in clubs and mutual interest associations than does the United States. Notes anthropologist Conrad P. Kottak,

"The typical American belongs to dozens of non-kin based groups. These include churches, political parties, clubs, teams, occupational groups, [and] organizations . . . In Brazil, where home and extended family hold their own so vigorously against the external world, non-kin associations are fewer" (Kottak 1990:166).

As we have seen, Brazilians are far more likely than Americans to live near and frequently visit family members. Given this emphasis on family, getting together with relative strangers to talk about gardening or great books or to plan a bake sale strikes Brazilians as odd indeed.

All of these considerations aside, in the end most Brazilians gave a simple down-to-earth explanation when queried about the lack of community *élan*. They said that they and most of their fellow immigrants were in New York for only one reason: to make as much money as fast as possible and return to Brazil. As such, immigrants do not anticipate being in the United States long enough to justify putting their scant time and energy into local groups of any kind. Moreover, to join a club or an organization might be a sign of permanence, evidence that they were really intending to stay in the United States, a proposition that most Brazilians reject. One Brazilian put it in no uncertain terms: "We don't have an immigrant spirit because we are *not* immigrants." Not seeing themselves as immigrants, Brazilians do not identify with other immigrants. Cristina Martes, who studied Brazilians in Boston, notes "Brazilians don't identify with immigrants because, among other things, they see themselves in a condition of temporary workers... whose objective is to make as much money in the United States as possible in order to return to Brazil..." (1995b:66).

Moreover, despite the ringing charges that Brazilians make against each other, many immigrants acknowledge the help they receive from their compatriots and recognize that the strident discourse about a community on the brink of implosion is overstated. Nearly all the Brazilian immigrants I talked with said they had gotten their start in the city with the assistance of Brazilian friends or relatives; two-thirds had help finding a place to live and about half that number found jobs through their fellow co-ethnics. Even long after they come to New York, immigrant employment networks continue to function. They help Brazilians who lost jobs find other work or get new jobs with better wages or working conditions.

Brazilians rely on each other for play as much as for work. Parties, gatherings of friends, sports events or an evening out at a restaurant or club are typically all-Brazilian affairs. And evidence of at least sporadic community solidarity can be found in the tens of thousands of Brazilians from all over the northeastern United States who attend the annual Brazilian Independence Day Fair in early September in Manhattan's Little Brazil.[4] Then, too, whenever a Brazilian singer or musician or dance troupe plays in a New York club or gives a concert, there is invariably a large contingent of Brazilians in the audience noisily celebrating their ethnicity.

---

4. This festival, first held in 1985, features dozens of booths selling Brazilian food and drink, handicrafts, tapes, t-shirts, and all manner of items with Brazilian logos. Brazilian music blares from loudspeakers and the festival invariably ends with hundreds of merrymakers dancing the samba in the street.

Booths selling Brazilian products are features of the Brazilian Independence Day Fair and other festivals.

HAVING FAITH

A vibrant exception to the paucity of institutional structures in New York's Brazilian immigrant community are its churches. This is true in other centers of Brazilian immigration as well. One researcher in Boston found that the only institution that united Brazilians in that city were its ethnic churches, and dozens of churches with services in Portuguese minister to the spiritual needs of Brazilian immigrants in south Florida as well (Badgley 1994; Neto and Bernardes 1996).

In New York City churches with religious services in Portuguese—most led by Brazilian clerics—are well attended by the Brazilian faithful. Catholic mass is celebrated in Portuguese at two churches in Manhattan and one in Queens. There are also Baptist and Seventh Day Adventist Churches that meet the spiritual needs of Brazilians in the city, along with at least five Pentecostal churches; the number is uncertain since this denomination has been growing rapidly, opening new churches to accomodate converts in the immigrant community. Rounding out the religious mix are a Spiritist center, several local branches of the Universal Church of the Kingdom of God (*Igreja Universal do Reino de Dios*), a creed founded in Brazil in the late 1970s, Candomblé, a syncretic Afro-Brazilian religion, and *Seicho-No-Ié*, a sect imported to Brazil from Japan.

A little more than half of the Brazilian immigrants in my study attended religious services with some regularity and their doctrinal loyalties were similar to those found in Brazil. Nearly three-quarters were Catholic, 13 percent were *crentes* ("believers"), as Protestants are called in Brazil, and the rest were either unaffiliated or espoused other beliefs including Spiritism. Just as in Brazil, membership in evangelical churches has been growing among Brazilians in New York. Estimates suggest that the number of Protestants in Brazil increased four-fold between 1960 and 1990, with the greatest growth in evangelical churches like the Assembly of God (Mariz 1994). Nevertheless, despite the evangelical upsurge, the vast majority of Brazilians remain at least nominally Catholic, as do most Brazilian immigrants in New York City.

Prior to the late 1980s no Catholic Church in New York celebrated mass in Portuguese, but reflecting the city's growing Brazilian population, three churches in the city now minister to the needs of Brazilian Catholics. The establishment of the city's first mass for Portuguese-speakers at the Church of Our Lady of Perpetual Aid (*Nossa Senhora do Perpetuo Socorro*) in 1990 reflects the changing ethnic composition of New York's immigrant population. For well over a half century, Our Lady of Perpetual Aid had been a Czechoslovakian national parish, but as the descendants of the original Czech congregants moved out to the suburbs, attendance at mass declined sharply and the Archdiocese of New York considered closing the church for good. Learning of this, a long time Brazilian resident of the city began lobbying local Catholic authorities to institute a Portuguese mass, suggesting that with its dwindling congregation, Our Lady of Perpetual Aid would be a suitable site for such a service. Officials of the Catholic Archdiocese then contacted the Brazilian Consulate to inquire about the number of Brazilians living in the New York area. "About 60,000," they were told. Impressed by such a critical mass of potential churchgoers, New York's Archdiocese endorsed Portuguese-language services for the Brazilian faithful.

While New York is home to a growing community of Brazilian Catholics, it was also the site of a burgeoning number of evangelical churches with services in Portuguese, churches that Pope John Paul II has referred to as "the invasion of the sects" (Mariz

1994). Brazilian evangelicals have indeed become increasingly visible in the city's Brazilian community. For the first time at the 1993 Brazilian Independence Day Street Fair, a contingent of well over one hundred Brazilians—mostly young people—carried "Jesus Saves" signs and distributed literature for the Missionary Christian Church (*Igreja Missionaria Cristiana*), an evangelical denomination in Queens. Ever since, the adherents of one evangelical church or another have been clearly visible at the fair, fervently proclaiming their faith, handing out literature, and proselytizing the swarms of Brazilians from all over the northeastern United States who descend on New York for their annual celebration of ethnicity.

The growth of evangelical churches also has been noted by other observers of the Brazilian immigrant scene. Cristina Martes (1996) suggests that their appeal lies in a theology that exhorts work, applauds personal success and encourages economic mobility, doctrines that reinforce the predilections of most new immigrants. Moreover, Brazilian Pentecostal churches in Boston, she points out, provide for the material as well as the spiritual needs of their congregants. Their pastors often become involved in the lives of their immigrant disciples, giving them advice on immigration and employment problems, while the churches provide day care, free English classes, donated clothes, and help finding jobs. Writes Martes: "The manner in which the Protestant churches become the primordial locus of immigrant sociability is important to an understanding of the success of these churches among Brazilian immigrants, the vast majority of whom were Catholic before they emigrated" (1996:45).

Evangelical churches have been compared to spiritual cocoons, sanctuaries comprised of like-minded believers bound together by common moral codes and religious beliefs. These cocoons both sustain and help separate adherents from the alien and sometimes hostile world that surrounds those new to this country. The churches empower their followers by promising them not only a felicitous afterlife but a bountiful one in the here and now. As such, Pentecostalism may be interpreted as less an escape from the temporal world than as a pragmatic strategy for survival in it.

The encompassing spirituality of evangelical churchgoers is evident in New York's Brazilian community. Take the Pentecostal

Church (*Igreja Pentecostal*) in Brooklyn as a case in point. Although nearly all its members reside in Queens, several times a week they make the long trek by subway to Brooklyn to attend the church's Portuguese language services, Bible study classes and youth fellowship meetings. Once there, they are surrounded by a bevy of like-minded immigrants.

During services the Brazilian pastor exhorts the faithful to abjure drinking alcohol and smoking cigarettes, avoid dancing and secular music, remain pure, if single, and faithful, if married; girls and women are instructed to dress modestly. Church members are urged to socialize only with each other within a spiritual community, at services held in church and in private homes, at church dinners and other church sponsored events. Communal outings to the beach in summer were designed to help church members keep their distance from other Brazilians—Brazilians who do not adhere to Pentecostalism's strict precepts on smoking, drinking, modest dress and behavior.

While members of this congregation are told to avoid non-observant Brazilians, they are actively engaged with fellow believers, expressing pride in the mutual assistance they give one another in finding jobs and providing food, shelter, and financial aid in times of need. They made a point of telling me how different they were in this regard from their secular compatriots. As one churchgoer put it: "They say we Brazilians are not united, that we don't help each other. But you can see for yourself that's not true here!"

Another determinedly evangelical church—and one of Brazilian origin—is the immodestly named Universal Church (*Igreja Universal*), now with close to twenty houses of worship in the United States stretching from coast to coast, including five outposts in the greater New York metropolitan area. In its stress on success, particularly financial success, the theology of the Universal Church is similar to that of some other evangelical ministeries. According to one of the church's New York-based pastors, the church does not "promise salvation only after death, but we believe God also helps converts in this life. We have many testimonies of people who have prospered and whose prayers have been answered after joining the church." The focal point of the service I attended were prayers for better jobs and improved financial opportunities. Much of the sermon was a plea to help raise thousands of dollars for the church's then half-completed branch in Brooklyn.[5]

Although its first New York outpost opened in 1986—a time when Brazilian immigrants were flocking to the city in large numbers—the Universal Church has never focused on ministering to the local Brazilian expatriate community. In fact, its services are conducted in English or Spanish, not in Portuguese, and its cable TV program features Brazilian pastors preaching in "Portanhol," the fractured Spanish often spoken by native speakers of Portuguese.

The abiding goal of the Universal Church is to convert immigrants, but immigrants of all nationalities, not just those from Brazil. Brazilians, in fact, account for less than 20 percent of its New York congregants and the services I attended were heavily peppered with immigrants from the Caribbean and Central America, with just a handful of Brazilians among them. Branches of the church were established in New York because, said the local pastor, it is a "crossroads drawing people from all over the world and we hope that the church's converts there will start new congregations when they go back to their own countries." In essence, immigrant believers are potential seeds who, it is hoped, will plant the church's teachings in their homelands. Through this process, the church is trying to replicate the enormous success it has had in Brazil where over eight hundred branches have been established since its founding in 1977. Indeed, the Universal Church, which has been dubbed "the multinational of faith" and the "fast food of faith," now has outposts on all continents, with recent additions in Singapore and Indonesia (*Veja* 1995b). In a real sense, then, the Universal Church is a transnational church, one that seems well positioned to benefit from the permeability of international borders.

TIME OFF

While a few Brazilian immigrants, especially evangelicals, spend a good deal of time in church-related activities even during their

---

5. The Universal Church has received extended criticism in the Brazilian press as a cult-like organization whose main concern is its own financial success, primarily achieved through the monetary contributions of its converts (*Veja* 1995b).

early months in New York, most new immigrants' single-minded pursuit of the "little green things" leaves them precious little time for anything else. Leisure is not only a rare commodity among immigrants new to this country but, as Brazilians put it, "leisure costs a lot around here." Going out to a restaurant, the movies or a concert is expensive in a city like New York and leisure also can have hidden costs if it takes time away from work.

Still, as the months go by and Brazilians grow weary of their endless labors, guilt about not spending all their waking hours at work begins to ebb and every last dollar earned is no longer strictly earmarked for that condo in Rio or the small business in Minas Gerais. The gradual process by which immigrants start to think more about life in the host country and less about returning home has been described before (Piore 1979). As this new perspective slowly takes hold, many immigrants become less willing to spend countless hours slaving away at dead-end jobs, and more loath to put in over time or continue to hold down a second job. Working shorter hours they earn less money, but they spend a little more of it on leisure. Then the suggestions begin: "Let's go out to dinner" or "Why don't we get tickets to the Nascimento concert"[6] or "How about having some of our friends over for a party."

Nevertheless, even when they mellow somewhat and allow themselves a little more time for play, immigrants say that the long hours they continue to put in on the job mean that their social life in New York is a pale reflection of what it was in Brazil. *Cariocas* (natives of Rio) fondly recall the idyllic hours they used to spend drinking icy glasses of *chopp* (draft beer) at beach front cafés in Ipanema; *mineiros* (natives of Minas Gerais) reminisce about tranquil family picnics in the countryside; and *paulistas* (natives of São Paulo) recount tales of leisurely dinners with friends at one of that city's lively *churrascarias* (barbecue restaurants).

Immigrant social life in New York is a truncated version of what it was in Brazil because it is the rare Brazilian who totally abandons the idea of saving money for the eventual return home. Brazilians are far more likely to spend a quiet evening entertaining family and friends at home than going out for an expensive

---

6. Milton Nascimento is a well-known Brazilian singer who has given sold out concerts in New York's Radio City Music Hall.

"night on the town." While half of the Brazilians I interviewed said that they ate out at New York restaurants at least occasionally, only one-third had attended a concert (other than a free one) in the city, and less than one-fifth had ever been to a nightclub.

When they do go out, Brazilians tend to patronize restaurants and clubs that feature the food and music of their homeland. By the mid-1990s, New York had at least a dozen such establishments with several more in nearby suburbs. Immigrants generally avoid the tourist-oriented Brazilian restaurants in the vicinity of Manhattan's Little Brazil, preferring the less costly ones in Queens and Newark. A Brazilian-style *churrascaria a rodizio* ("barbecue in the round") in Queens, where waiters pass from table to table with large skewers of grilled beef, pork and chicken, is particularly popular with immigrants. The appeal of this cavernous eatery, which serves gargantuan amounts of food at reasonable prices, extends well beyond the Brazilian community; its diners mirror the striking ethnic rainbow of immigrant New York.

Aside from eating out, some immigrants also spend their hard earned dollars for concerts and shows with Brazilian artists. In the last few years many of that nation's best known entertainers—Caetano Veloso, Gal Costa, Milton Nascimento, Gilberto Gil, Maria Bethania, Beth Carvalho, Ivan Lins—have given concerts in the city or have appeared in New York clubs. And when Brazilian singers or musicians are featured in free open-air performances like Summerstage in Central Park, the extent and verve of the city's Brazilian population becomes apparent. Hordes of Brazilian immigrants inevitably turn out to sing and shout and dance to the music and cheer on their compatriots in joyous observance of their common ethnicity.

Warm weather means outings to one of the metropolitan area's beaches as well as get-togethers for cookouts and picnics in urban parks. Summer excursions to the seashore are especially popular among *cariocas* who pine for Rio's famed beaches. Brazilians say they can always spot knots of their compatriots at the seashore because Brazilian women are the only ones clad in *tangas*, the tiny string bikinis manufactured in Brazil that have become a ubiquitous symbol of Rio de Janeiro and its "Girl from Ipanema."

While Brazilians go to the beach or city parks or occasionally dine out or go to shows, informal gatherings at home are by far the most common modes of social interaction in the immigrant community. Indeed, some Brazilians get together with the same group of friends week in and week out. They might drink *caipirinhas* or beer or have a *feijoada,* or perhaps watch the latest installment of a Brazilian *telenovela* (soap opera) on the VCR, or roll up the rug and do the *lambada,* a Brazilian dance craze of the early 1990s.[7] Parties are also given to mark special occasions in the lives of immigrants, to celebrate a birth or marriage, for example, or to bid a boisterous farewell to a compatriot returning to Brazil.

Futebol (soccer)—that quintessentially Brazilian sport—is also a favored pastime in the community. Almost a quarter of the Brazilian men in my study played *futebol* at least occasionally, although only about one in ten were members of organized soccer teams. Some of the teams have regularly scheduled games, say every Saturday morning weather permitting, but others play only sporadically. The soccer teams are either all-Brazilian affairs, like the Athletic Club of Minas Gerais, or of mixed nationality. The relatively modest numbers involved in soccer teams belie the singular role that *futebol* plays in the Brazilian community both as a major spectator sport and a signature of shared identity. Many immigrants of all ages and both sexes regularly attend soccer games played by their compatriots. For example, on Memorial and Labor Day weekends several hundred Brazilians cheer from the sidelines as Brazilian soccer teams compete at an outdoor playing field in Manhattan. These sporting events have a distinctly Brazilian flair. Spectators are dressed in green and gold—Brazil's national colors—Brazilian flags flutter in the wind and street vendors sell *salgadinhos* and *guaraná,* Brazilian snacks and soft drinks.

The true significance of this sport as a symbol of Brazilian national identity was only brought home to me when the World Cup games in soccer were played in the United States in the summer of 1994. American newspaper and TV commentators often noted the heady exuberance of Brazilian fans, immigrants and

---

7. *Caipirinhas* are potent drinks made of Brazilian cane alcohol, sugar and freshly squeezed limes. *Feijoada* (literally "big bean") is the Brazilian national dish. It consists of assorted meats simmered in black beans and served with rice, kale, orange slices, toasted manioc flour and hot sauce.

Samba and soccer (*futebol*) as symbols of Brazilian ethnicity provide the name for this street stall at the Brazilian Independence Day Fair.

visitors alike, as Brazil became the first nation ever to win its fourth World Cup. They were *tetracampeões*, "four-time champions" as headlined in the sports page of the *New York Times*. From New York to California, in what was typically the first media coverage ever of Brazilians immigrants in the United States, accounts of carnival-like street parades and crowds of wildly enthusiastic fans made the news. In northern California, for example, where Brazil's winning team played most of its games, the local news media suddenly discovered San Francisco's large Brazilian community for the first time.

All over the United States in cities with sizeable Brazilian populations, Brazilians celebrated their victory with vivacious abandon (Longman 1994; *New York Times*, July 18, 1994). In Washington D.C. after Brazil beat the Netherlands in the quarter finals, the Brazilian crowd that had been jammed into a local Brazilian restaurant to watch the game on a big screen TV spilled out into the street, dancing the samba and blocking traffic as dozens of their compatriots drove by, horns honking and cars festooned with Brazilian flags. In New York's Little Brazil, before the start of the final game, throngs of Brazilian fans milled about. A large TV screen had been placed curbside in front of a store selling Brazilian products and street vendors hawked beer and soft drinks. Within a half hour of Brazil's World Cup triumph over Italy, hordes of Brazilians arrived from Queens pouring out of subway stations to join the raucous open-air celebration already in progress. Groups playing *batucada,* Afro-Brazilian percussion music, shared the packed street with lines of samba dancers, some in very skimpy attire. There were also people wrapped in large Brazilian flags wearing extravagant green and yellow wigs atop their heads, a man walking on stilts and several garishly dressed Brazilian drag queens. A line of New York police officers stood by with a dazed look in their eyes, scratching their heads, as if to say: "What's going on here? Who are these people and where did they come from?" evidence of the on-going invisibility of this immigrant community, is a topic to which we now turn.

5

Ethnicity, Race and Gender

The police officers on duty at the celebration of Brazil's World Cup victory are not the only New Yorkers unaware of this new immigrant stream. Theirs is a "secret, silent migration," as one Brazilian put it, since almost no one outside their own community knows about it. Brazilians are truly an invisible minority because of Americans' confusion about who they are and what language they speak. Moreover, Little Brazil Street notwithstanding, Brazilian invisibility also results from the lack of a tangible community in the city, a locale tinged with its own distinct ethnicity like Chinatown or Little Italy, or even a residential neighborhood Brazilians could call their own. Nor is it a surprise that hardly any New Yorkers are aware of Little Brazil's existence since the Brazilian enterprises on this Manhattan street are interspersed with restaurants and businesses of many nationalities, muting the Brazilian presence there.

Brazilians are also unknown to most New Yorkers because they have received almost no news coverage. The first mention of the city's Brazilian community in the *New York Times*, for example, was in an article on the sport's page about the noisy enthusiasm of local Brazilian fans during the World Cup games (Longman 1994). The only other news about Brazilian immigrants was published a year later when the murder of a Brazilian jogger in Central Park made the front page and the paper did a brief background story on the community entitled "Slaying Shocks Usually Upbeat Brazilians" (Lee 1995). Then, too, since Brazilians do not work in sweatshops, they have not been the targets of headline-making raids by United States immigration agents.

Brazilians are also absent from media coverage of the new immigrant groups that are making New York's ethnic and linguistic mosaic ever more complex. A case in point. When the Ellis Island Museum in New York harbor opened, the city's role as the premiere immigrant gateway to this country was highlighted and the New York media ran stories about many of the city's recent immigrant groups. A one-hour prime time TV special covered the new wave of migration and featured clips or mentioned immigrants from at least fifteen countries, but not from Brazil. Likewise, in a magazine cover story about the intricate medley of ethnic groups that comprise New York, thirty-two different nationalities were cited including Argentines, Cambodians, Thais, Guatemalans, Trinidadians, and "forty or fifty Laotian families living in the Bronx." Brazilians were not in the mix (Brenner 1991).

The invisibility of Brazilian immigrants is not limited to popular consciousness and the mass media; they are also difficult to find in reports based on official statistics. A *USA Today* article based on the 1990 census listed the top forty immigrant groups in the United States. An accompanying chart included "immigrant groups larger than 100,000." In 40th place are Thais with about 107,000 fellow ethnics in the United States Even Hondurans and Hungarians are said to out distance Brazilians in number (Usdansky 1993). Brazilians, of course, do not appear on the list because, as we have seen, the 1990 census managed to count only 94,000 of them in the entire country!

What is all the more surprising about the on-going invisibility of this burgeoning ethnic colony is that it is unaffected by the growing popularity of all things Brazilian. Over the last decade, clubs featuring Brazilian music or performers or concerts with Brazilian musicians have become a ubiquitous part of New York night life. Trendy restaurants featuring both real and faux Brazilian cuisine while not quite legion, are highly popular. Brazil was even called "the nation *du jour* among New York style-setters" by *New York Magazine*. This is why Brazilian food and music have received abundant coverage in the pages of the *New York Times* and other media outlets. But this interest and exposure has not extended to the Brazilian immigrant community itself. Part of the explanation lies in Americans' ignorance about "our southern neighbors," most especially Brazil. But it also rests on Brazilian ethnicity as a contested category.

AMERICAN IGNORANCE

In the United States, Latin America is often portrayed as "just one civilization artificially divided into different countries" (Sims 1995:4E). The vast majority of Americans, even educated ones, have no idea that Brazil is in any way different from the rest of Latin America. Just one example: After consulting with a physician in New York City—a highly trained specialist in his field—on a minor medical matter, I mentioned that I was going to Brazil to teach for a semester at a university in Rio de Janeiro. "Oh," he said, "you must be very fluent in Spanish." "No, actually, I am not," I replied. "But I do speak Portuguese." This illustrates the problem. Despite the size of Brazil (about 160 million people) and its importance (the eighth largest economy in the world), most Americans know very little about Brazil, including the fact that Brazilians speak Portuguese. They think that Spanish is the language of Brazil and that Portuguese is spoken only in Portugal.

American confusion about Brazilian language and ethnicity dates back decades, at least to the era of the "Brazilian bombshell" Carmen Miranda who, at one point during the 1940s, was the highest paid movie actress in the United States. Her elaborate kitschy costumes with flouncy skirts and bare midriff topped off by a monumental fruit-laden headdress and an exaggerated accent helped shape American perceptions of Brazil and Brazilians. Miranda became the generic "Latina" whose movies were set indistinguishably in Cuba and Mexico as well as in Brazil. She represented an undifferentiated "south of the border" reality to many Americans.

Brazilian immigrants decry American ignorance of their land and language. As one immigrant put it: "Americans have very little culture when it comes to Latin America." Stories about American naiveté are legion in New York's Brazilian community and were recounted to me with a mixture of hilarity and chagrin. A popular one concerned the benighted American who telephoned the Brazilian Consulate seeking tourist information about Buenos Aires. Another was about the American who asked a Brazilian immigrant, "Just what kind of Spanish do you speak?" After she replied that she was from Brazil and did *not* speak Spanish, the American said, "Oh, of course, you're from Brazil. That's the country where the upper class speaks Portuguese and the lower class speaks Spanish." As one Brazilian who was barely able to contain his frustration put it: "There are 300 million Portuguese-speakers in the world today and I find it just incredible that Americans don't know there is a difference between our language and Spanish."

Brazilians told other tales of the American penchant for reducing the rich complexity that is Brazil to a simplistic duality. In the American imagination, Brazil is typecast in one of two ways. It is either the land of white, sparkling beaches—the girl from Ipanema-sultry mulatto-string bikini-samba stereotype, or the home of the vast impenetrable Amazon—the lush, primitive tropical forest cliché. The latter image is evident in the following anecdotes. An immigrant from São Paulo, a modern metropolis of some 14 million people, was questioned about the "Indians roaming" the streets of his city. Another Brazilian said that Americans regularly asked her inane questions like, "Do you eat snakes?" "Do you have windows in your houses?" Americans, she said, "think we live in huts. It's disappointing because I thought Americans were so cultured and they don't even know where Brazil is!" One Brazilian expressed annoyance that many U.S. Hispanics are also ignorant about Brazil and cited a Spanish language publication that listed the capital of Brazil as Rio de Janeiro—Brasília has been the capital for nearly four decades. "If Americans . . . think that Brazil is in Bolivia, okay. But when our Mexican, Cuban, Puerto Rican and other Hispanic friends commit the same insanities . . . why it's pathetic" (quoted in *News from Brazil* 1990). This was a mocking reference to former President Ronald Reagan's blunder on a trip to Brazil. At a state dinner in his honor he raised his glass and made a toast to Bolivia!

WHAT IS A BRAZILIAN?

Among newly arrived Brazilian immigrants in the United States, American ignorance of Brazil and American categorizations of ethnicity both contribute to a new consciousness of what it means to be Brazilian. They also present Brazilians with a dilemma, as in the following case: On most U.S. employment forms, job applicants are asked to indicate their race and ethnic group. A typical category is: "Hispanic from Mexico, Central America or South America." Even though Brazilians are from South America, they cannot check this category because they are not Hispanic since the term refers to Spanish-speakers or those of Spanish-speaking descent and, as we know, Brazilians speak Portuguese. So Brazilians are South Americans; they are also Latin Americans (*Latinos*), but they are *not* Hispanics.[1]

Like some other immigrant groups in the United States, Brazilians contest or, at least, sidestep, American racial and ethnic categorizations (Basch, Glick Schiller and Szanton Blanc 1994; Gonzalez 1992). One of the first things that Brazilian immigrants learn to say after they arrive in New York is: "We are *not* Hispanic and we don't speak Spanish!" There are several reasons why Brazilian immigrants strongly object to being labeled Hispanic. Brazilians try to distinguish themselves linguistically and culturally from other Latin American immigrant groups in New York partly because of cultural pride, what they see as the uniqueness of their "race"(*raça*). This attitude, in turn, has deep roots in Brazil, a nation with a keen sense of its own distinctiveness from the rest of the continent. Brazilians have long been indifferent to other Latin American nations, dismissing their common Iberian heritage as of little importance. As such, Brazilians lack a common identity either with other South Americans or with Hispanics in general. In fact, the term "Hispanic" (*hispano*) does not even exist in Brazil. There "Spanish" refers to people from Spain, while citizens of Spanish-speaking countries in Latin America are called Mexicans, Chileans, Peruvians, Argentines and so on.

Most Brazilians believe that Americans treat them better when they make it clear that they are not Hispanic. They insist that Hispanics are discriminated against in the United States and that when Americans confuse them with Hispanics, they too suffer from anti-Hispanic bias. Brazilians' efforts to disassociate them-

---

1. Latino, meaning a person from Latin America, is a more inclusive term than Hispanic. Although all Hispanics are Latinos, not all Latinos are Hispanic.

selves from Hispanics also grow out of their own prejudice and feelings of superiority over the city's other Latin American immigrant groups. I heard many disparaging remarks about Hispanics during the course of my research. I was told, for example, that "Americans don't know that we Brazilians are different from Hispanics...that Brazilians are very hard workers." Such attitudes are rooted in the comparatively elite social status of Brazilian immigrants. Since the vast majority of Brazilians in New York are from the middle strata of Brazilian society and many are well educated, they consider it an insult to be confused with the rest of the city's Latino population, a large portion of which is poorer and has had less education than they. A few Brazilians even object to being called "Latino," although it is an accurate designation since it refers to individuals from Latin America without reference to the language they speak. Nevertheless, Brazilians dislike the term because they believe it carries the dual stigmas of prejudice and low socio-economic status.

The antipathy toward being identified with other Latin Americans is not limited to Brazilians in the United States. In similar fashion, Brazilians of Japanese descent who have emigrated to Japan take offense at being confused with Peruvians of Japanese descent living there and assume an air of superiority to immigrants of Japanese heritage from other Latin American nations[2]. "The Peruvian is lazy," opined a Japanese-Brazilian. "I detest being called *nambeijin* (South American) by the Japanese because I don't want to be put in the same group as the Peruvians and Argentines..." (quoted in Chigusa 1994:48).

There is one final twist to this complex pirouette of ethnic identity. While many Brazilian immigrants in New York are angered when they are confused with Hispanics, glorying in their cultural and linguistic distinctiveness, a few Brazilians—usually those who have been in this country for several years—do not want to be identified with their own compatriots either. These are the same immigrants who talk about avoiding other Brazilians

---

2. About 170,000 Japanese-Brazilians have emigrated to Japan since the mid-1980s (Linger 1995). They are there for the same reason other Brazilians have gone to the United States: to take jobs that pay far more than any they could get in Brazil.

and spurning them as friends, part of the "you can't trust Brazilians in the United States" discourse that was discussed in the last chapter. One researcher has labeled this the "Brazilian paradox" (Badgeley 1994), the regrettable situation in which Brazilians insist on maintaining their separateness from other ethnic groups, while also remaining emotionally distant from one another.

THEY WERE NOT COUNTED

The undercount of Brazilians in the 1990 United States Census was one practical consequence of their enigmatic ethnicity. Only a fraction of Brazilians were counted or, if they were counted, their nationality was not specified. The actual number of Brazilians living in New York City and elsewhere in the United States who were missed in the census enumeration is unknown but, as we have seen, the undercount may have been as high as 80 percent for the country as a whole.

The undercount of Brazilians is a direct outgrowth of the census categories used. "Brazil" does not appear on the census form even though nearly every other country in Latin America is listed. Citizens from one of the few countries not named can check the box marked "Yes, other Spanish/Hispanic" and fill in the blank with their country of origin. But, as we know, Brazilians are not Hispanics and they vehemently reject being designated as such. Many Brazilians who were willing to fill out the census forms did not do so because of the limitations of the ethnic categories provided. They wanted to state their nationality but were annoyed that the only way they could do so was to check the box marked "Spanish/Hispanic" and then write in "Brazilian."

Restrictive ethnic categories were not the only reason many Brazilians did not participate in the 1990 census. Fear also played a part. Many undocumented Brazilians were afraid to fill out the forms because they did not believe that census information was confidential and felt certain that it would be turned over to the immigration authorities. Apathy was more important still. A number of Brazilian immigrants told me that they and their compatriots did not send in the forms because "we couldn't care less about the census." After all, they reminded me, most Brazilians are in the United States only for the short-term and have no interest in being counted (Margolis 1995a).

THE COLOR SPECTRUM

Brazilian immigrants in New York often talk about being confused with Hispanics and about the peculiarity of American ethnic designations. They also discuss many other issues that touch on their identity in the United States; their invisibility as a distinct ethnic group, the lack of unity among their fellow Brazilians and the social class and education of their immigrant compatriots. But, I rarely heard them discuss a related subject: race and race relations within the Brazilian community.

We already know that the racial make-up of the Brazilian immigrant population in New York is weighted towards the lighter side of the color spectrum, making it atypical of Brazil as a nation. Eighty percent of the Brazilians in my study were white, 8 percent were light mulatto or mulatto, and 8 percent were black. In all, people of color appeared to account for about 16 percent of New York's Brazilian community, a far cry from the 1990 census figure of nearly 45 percent reported for Brazil as a whole (*Fundação Instituto Brasileiro de Geografia e Estatística* 1994). The racial composition of New York's Brazilian population was corroborated both by Brazilian immigrants themselves and by my own observations at many large gatherings of Brazilians—street fairs, sports events, concerts, and the like—during the course of my field research. Brazilians of color, including blacks and mulattos, typically comprised 10 percent or less of those in attendance.

Ironically, although Brazilians of color are underrepresented in New York's immigrant population, white Brazilians seem to interact more with their black and mulatto compatriots in the United States than they do in Brazil (Ehrlich 1990). This is not as contradictory as it appears, however, because social interaction is generally influenced more by social class than by race. In other words, Brazilians of similar socio-economic status tend to socialize with each other and since Brazilians in New York, including Brazilians of color, are mostly from the middle strata of Brazilian society, white middle-class immigrants are more likely to have contact with their black and brown brothers and sisters in New York than they do in Brazil.

The greater social interaction between Brazilians of all racial hues in New York helps reduce the heavy baggage of racial stereotyping that some white Brazilians bring with them to this country. That white Brazilians are more likely to see people of color in middle-class positions in the United States than they did in Brazil also plays a role in reducing prejudice. Said one immigrant:

> "I think that racial attitudes towards blacks change for all Brazilians who come to the United States. In Brazil you don't see [blacks eating] in restaurants, and here you do. At the beginning it's difficult to accept this idea because we are not accustomed to this. We grew up in a society that has more blacks than whites, but blacks have always lived under very bad conditions in Brazil. What changed was my perception of the Negro race. I respect them for what they've achieved here" (quoted in Ehrlich 1989:62).

When Brazilian immigrants talk about race, one common element in their discourse is how "different" African Americans are from people of color in Brazil. White Brazilians contrast what they perceive as the "aggressiveness" of black Americans with the submissive behavior they had come to expect from Afro-Brazilians back home. But they are confusing race and class. In Brazil, people from the lower echelons of society are expected to act with deference and respect towards those higher up on the social ladder. Because Afro-Brazilians are disproportionately found in the lower strata of Brazilian society, Brazilians conflate such behavior with skin color and are "surprised" when African Americans do not behave in a similarly deferential manner.

GENDER SNAPSHOTS

Like racial stereotypes, gender role traditions also soften under the sway of migration. To cite one pertinent example: although women are traditionally seen as migrating for family reasons—to join a male breadwinner or to reunite the family—my own and other research challenges this common notion (Simon and DeLey 1986; Zentgraf 1995)). Less than one-third of the Brazilian women I studied were married at the time I interviewed them, and even fewer were married when they first arrived in the United States. In other words, contrary to conventional wisdom, family considerations did not spur most of these women to migrate to the United States. In fact, I found that Brazilian women came to New York for exactly the same reason that Brazilian men did—to take jobs that paid far more than any they could ever find back home.

When women migrate abroad to seek work, gendered labor recruitment is often involved. That is, the particular labor market needs of specific cities in the United States or other host countries may require more female (or male) migrants (Repak 1995). For example, male immigrants might readily find employment in a certain locale if workers for low-wage construction jobs were in demand there. Domestic service is another case of gendered labor recruitment since the call for live-in housekeepers, day maids, nannies and babysitters is almost entirely a demand for *female* labor.

Employment in this sector of the labor market may have given immigrant women an advantage of sorts. Since 1986 when the U.S. Congress passed the Immigration Reform and Control Act tightening penalties on employees who hire undocumented workers, immigrant women have been able to find work somewhat more easily than immigrant men. The reason is that employers of babysitters, housekeepers, and nannies are less likely than others to ask about their employee's legal status or to require that they have a green card (Repak 1995).

NEW LAND, NEW ROLES

Whether they work as nannies, maids, street vendors or gogo dancers, Brazilian women's employment is the primary catalyst for shifts in gender roles. What is crucial is the earning power of women immigrants, not the type of job they hold. Women's greater financial autonomy is what sets the stage for a reformulation of traditional Brazilian gender roles. Many immigrant women, particularly married women, contend that their former dependence is replaced by the "executive power" (*poder executivo*) they acquire from their new role as breadwinners. They take jobs and for the first time in their lives they earn as much or even more than their husbands. And this, in turn, gives them more familial decision-making power. Indeed, I found no evidence that the conventional Brazilian world view that the street (*a rua*) is a male preserve and the home (*a casa*) a female's negated the power bestowed by women's financial contribution to the household (Da Matta 1991).

To be sure, Brazilian women are not unique in their new found independence as international migrants. Other research has cited the effects of paid employment on women's status and role within the context of international migration (Pessar 1985; Haines 1986; Hondagneu-Sotelo 1994). A study of the migration of Dominicans to New York, for example, noted that since immigrant wages in the city were low—at least in the early years of migration—most Dominican households were incapable of maintaining the traditional male-wage earner/female-dependent division of labor. Men's wages simply were insufficient to support a household, making it essential that women contribute to basic living expenses (Grasmuck and Pessar 1992). Similarly, Haitian women who held jobs in New York were found to have far greater economic autonomy than they had back home, particularly women who had not been employed in Haiti or whose earnings only supplemented their husband's (Buchanan 1979). Along the same lines, Jamaican women spoke of the "independence" and "financial control" that migration to New York afforded them. Central American women in Los Angeles were said to feel "more independent in the United States" because they had more options, particularly in terms of wage labor, than they did back home (Foner 1986; Chinchilla and Hamilton 1995). All of these studies suggest, then, that a realignment of economic responsibilities can moderate the time-worn patriarchal ideology that asserts men should be a family's lone or, at least, its primary breadwinner.

But women's greater autonomy within the context of migration sometimes comes at a price. While women's employment lessens their dependence on men and may enhance self-confidence, research suggests that women's new financial authority also can lead to greater discord between the sexes, particularly among wives and husbands. Ironically, for some immigrant women the achievement of economic parity has not led to more egalitarian households but to the break up of their marriages (Grasmuck and Pessar 1992). Here is a case in point from my own research on Brazilian immigrants in New York City. It illustrates just how a reordering of traditional roles can transform lives and gender relations:

Veronica and Claudio had been married for ten years. They had one son and lived in an apartment in Astoria, Queens. They had been living in New York for two years when I met them and both had jobs cleaning apartments. Veronica was earning somewhat more than Claudio and she purchased whatever she pleased with her wages—a dining room table, a color TV set—without consulting Claudio. On weekends Veronica often went out with friends to restaurants and nightclubs. Claudio, who preferred to spend his time listening to his large CD collection, stayed home with their son.

This lifestyle contrasted sharply with what they were used to in Brazil. Claudio was an assistant bank manager there as well as the lone family breadwinner and Veronica was a full-time housewife. Having no income of her own, Veronica never made a major purchase without her husband's approval. On weekends Claudio went out with his friends to bars or to the beach, while Veronica stayed home with their young son. She would make dinner and sometimes Claudio came home to eat it, other times he would not.

After several months in New York Veronica was clearly enjoying her heady new financial independence and the partial reversal of her family's traditional division of labor. Claudio was far less pleased. At this point, Veronica began telling Claudio that he was simply "paying for his past sins" in Brazil—not showing up for dinner, going out with his friends and leaving her at home. As a result of these role shifts, a great deal of friction was evident between the two. They have since divorced and Veronica, who continues to live with her son in Queens, is now married to an American of Puerto Rican ancestry. Claudio has returned to Brazil.

A number of Brazilians told me that this scenario was not uncommon and that many marriages broke up after couples moved to New York. Most credited the break ups to the fact that married women were far more likely to be employed in the United States than they were in Brazil and that with a job came greater economic autonomy and a renegotiation of traditional gender roles. One Brazilian even told a friend who had just arrived in New York that, if he valued his marriage, he should discourage his wife from going to work. He then bet him that they would get divorced if she took a job. She went to work at a restaurant and, indeed, within two months they separated.

This case and that of Veronica and Claudio point to one factor that seems to be critical in a couple's willingness and ability to moderate conventional gender roles: whether or not they married or began living together before or after they came to the United States. Brazilian immigrants suggested that couples who meet in New York and then marry are less likely to wind up separated or divorced than those who were married before leaving Brazil. In New York, the reasoning goes, the woman was already employed when the couple first met, so her work and the economic clout that goes with it was a given from the start of the relationship. This seems to be true of Brazilian immigrants in Boston as well, since evidence suggests that divorce rates are higher among couples who emigrated there together. Said one member of Boston's Brazilian immigrant community:

> "To tell the truth there are many separations between couples here. These couples aren't able to stay together because it is so liberal here. In Brazil, the man works and the woman stays home. It is rare that a woman works. Here a woman has to work just like a man and everything is split up. It seems that people become...I don't know...selfish. I think that here everyone has equal rights and this brings on many problems" (quoted in Badgley 1994:84–85).

The time and place of marriage also may play a critical role in the explosive issue of the household division of labor—who cleans, who makes dinner and washes the dishes, and who takes care of the kids, if there are any. Social class and education also seem to affect the domestic division of labor. Research suggests that better educated couples who are both employed come closer to an "egalitarian model of conjugal relations" than do those with less education and a dependent spouse (Safa 1995:46).

The renegotiation of who does what at home can be a volatile question that impacts the health and longevity of marital and other intimate relationships. A Brazilian woman said that while her boyfriend "never did anything domestic back in Brazil," he had changed quite a lot since immigrating to the United States and they now had a more equitable division of labor at home. One male immigrant noted his own updated ideology:

> "You lose a lot of preconceived notions about the relationship between men and women. Here in the United States, the man participates more in the life of the house and the woman has much more dialogue with the husband. The man allows (sic) the woman to work out of necessity. A man who helps the woman in domestic chores

begins to appreciate what housework is like and he gives it more value."

Once again, studies of other immigrant groups in the United States suggest parallels with the Brazilian case. For example, Salvadoran women in Washington D.C. who formed attachments to men after migration were somewhat more successful in getting them to participate in domestic work than those whose relationships predated their arrival in this country (Repak 1995). Jamaican men were more likely to "help" their wives with housework and child care in New York than they were back home and many Jamaican immigrants, both male and female, began questioning "the legitimacy of the traditional division of labor that assigns only women to housework" (Foner 1986:152). And when women from the Dominican Republic who had moved to New York were asked how relations between husbands and wives had improved since leaving home, the response was a more equitable division of household responsibilities. For most of these women, in fact, an "improvement in gender relations had been an unintended outcome of the immigrant experience" (Grasmuck and Pessar 1992:155). It is precisely this "improvement" in gender relations that makes some Brazilian immigrant women reluctant to return home. What, they wonder, will become of the greater equality they enjoyed in New York? What will happen to the increased freedom and autonomy that comes with a paycheck once they are back in Brazil?

6

From Sojourner to Settler

"A person really can be successful in Brazil," opined Pedro, the husband in the popular Brazilian soap opera *Patria Minha* ("My Homeland"). Pedro and his wife Esther, both immigrants in New York, were arguing about their future and whether or not they should return to Brazil. "No, you can't," Esther shot back with some vehemence, "Brazil is corruption, it's hunger, it's...I don't know. It's just *not* a place where you can really succeed." Some real life variation of this fictional conversation is doubtlessly repeated over and over again in the homes of Brazilian immigrants in New York and elsewhere in the United States. But the decision of immigrants to stay in this country or return home is not nearly so clear cut and simple as it may appear. Moreover, even when a decision is "final," it is sometimes reversed. Take the case of Huberto, a Brazilian immigrant who had lived in New York for about five years. After much thought and some uncertainty, he finally decided to give up his apartment and his job managing a popular coffee bar in Manhattan and return home to São Paulo "for good." Yet, less than six weeks after going back to Brazil, Humberto's compatriot and co-worker at the coffee bar told me that Huberto had phoned from Brazil saying he had been unable to find a decent job and was discouraged by the economic situation he found there. As a result, he had already booked a flight and was planning to return to New York in several weeks.

OUR HEADS ARE IN TWO PLACES

Many factors come into play in the initial resolve to stay or to go and the decision is almost never an easy one. The picture is particularly murky for Brazilian immigrants because, unlike many immigrant groups who arrive in the United States determined to make a new life in this country, most Brazilians come here with the sole intention of making a new life *back home*. That is, they are only in New York or Boston or Miami to make money for the return to Brazil. At least initially, then, Brazilians see themselves as sojourners rather than as settlers. Sojourners maintain their orientation toward their own country; they are little engaged with the host society and they live for the day they can go home (Chavez 1988). Sojourners are literally people between two worlds; they live in a state of "in-betweenness" (Basch, Glick Schiller, Szanton Blanc 1994:8). As Brazilians in New York often put it: "We are here, but our heads [or hearts] are in Brazil." In a real sense, they are torn between their material and their emotional needs.

Brazilians, in essence, become transnational migrants, people who sustain familial, cultural and economic ties that ignore international borders and span the home and the host societies (Basch, Glick Schiller, and Szanton Blanc 1994). The dual orientation of Brazilians and other transnational migrants is partly dependent on modern communication and transportation networks. Rapid transmission of news, sports and culture via television, videotape, fax and telephone allows transnational migrants to stay in touch with what is happening back home. Brazilian immigrants in New York, for example, generally know more about news and sports scores in Brazil than in the United States. In fact, they are able to stay remarkably up-to-date about events in their homeland (Margolis 1995b). Be it the latest soap opera, soccer match, carnival extravaganza or political scandal, Brazilian immigrants in the United States often have access within days of the event. In New York, Miami, and Los Angeles they can buy video tapes of the latest *telenovela* (soap opera) hit on TV Globo, Brazil's largest television network, and in Boston, a Brazilian newspaper publishes a weekly summary of the twists and turns of the plots of popular evening soap operas.

The immigrant community's appetite for Brazilian news and entertainment has not gone unnoticed by Brazil's technologically sophisticated broadcast industry. One Brazilian television network produces a weekly half hour program in New York that features Brazilian music, sports clips, interviews with Brazilian politicians, and direct feeds from the network's nightly news broadcast in Brazil. The show is carried on cable television stations in five U.S. markets that have sizeable Brazilian immigrant populations.

Brazilian immigrants also stay in touch with their homeland through occasional visits. Whether or not immigrants travel to Brazil themselves depends on how long they have been in the United States and, more importantly, on their legal status. The general rule is, the longer Brazilians have lived in this country, the better the odds are that they have a green card, and the more likely it is that they have gone back to Brazil to visit. A green card allows an immigrant to come and go from the United States at will as long as the stay abroad is less than one year. Despite the recency of this migration stream and its high percentage of undocumented immigrants, well over half the Brazilians in my study had gone home for a visit at least once since arriving in this country. Slightly fewer have had friends or relatives from Brazil come to the United States to visit them.

By far the most constant means of contact with relatives and friends back home is via telephone, although a few immigrants also used Camcorders to send video-taped messages to Brazil about their New York activities. Nearly all Brazilians in my study called home on a regular basis and they spent a lot of money to do so. Monthly phone bills of $80 to $150 were common, while a few immigrants sheepishly admitted that their bills reached $200 a month or more. AT&T apparently has realized what good customers they have in Brazilian immigrants. A "phone home" advertising campaign suggested that "long distance calls to Brazil are easier than a one-note samba," an allusion to the classic Brazilian lyric. An illustration of how readily Brazilians call home follows: When I was in a home furnishing store in Manhattan and asked the Brazilian owner, a long time resident of New York City, how to say "wine rack" in Portuguese, he was disturbed when he could not recall the phrase. As quickly as one might consult a dictionary, he dialed Brazil to ask a friend.

Sending money home is another sign of sojourner status as well as a major incentive for transnational migration. Frequent remittances indicate a close association and identification with the home community as well as a higher probability of return. Just over half of the Brazilians in my New York study sent money home. Most immigrants sent remittances to their parents; only about 20 percent sent them to spouses and children. Much of the money sent to Brazil by immigrants was actually for their own future use there. Savings might be earmarked for buying a house or apartment, starting a business, or making a major purchase or investment. For the most part, then, Brazilian immigrants in New York City again do not conform to prevailing stereotypes, that of the undocumented alien struggling to send money back home to sustain an impoverished family.

To Stay or To Go

Given that the vast majority of Brazilian immigrants are sojourners, not settlers, when they arrive in New York, the decision to stay in the United States is an about face for most of them; it is a change of their original plan. What are the factors that go into such a major decision? Timing is one. As the length of stay in the United States increases, it becomes ever more difficult to return home since "it implies starting all over again in Brazil" (Martes 1995b:9). Length of stay, in turn, often correlates with legal status which also affects the decision to stay or to go. With some exceptions, the longer immigrants have lived in this country, the more likely they are to have green cards, and the greater the likelihood they will not go back to Brazil to live.

The decision to stay in the United States comes at a different time in the lives of immigrants than the initial decision to migrate. They are older and often have families; providing better opportunities for their children can be a powerful motive for remaining in this country. Children, especially teenagers, who have spent years in the United States also may express their reluctance to go back to a country they hardly know. And, having lived in the United States, immigrants have more information about what life is like here and what the option of returning to Brazil entails. Some stay for the simple reason that they want to maintain the standard of living they have grown used to in the United States.

Gender also can be an important variable in the stay-or-go equation. Although no studies have been done after Brazilians return home, the findings on other immigrant groups are suggestive. Some immigrant women in New York's Dominican community were reluctant to go home because they knew their nation's division of labor by gender and social class made their employment prospects dim. In order to delay the departure from New York, some Dominican women bought expensive durable goods like furniture and large household items. "This strategy serves both to root the family securely and comfortably in the United States and to deplete the funds needed to relocate," note the researchers who conducted the study (Grasmuck and Pessar 1992:156). Moreover, many of the immigrant women who did return to the Dominican Republic said they were dissatisfied with traditional gender roles there, missed paid employment, and resented their renewed economic dependence on their husbands. Similarly, a study of returned migrants in Ireland, Newfoundland, and Barbados revealed that after the return home, women were significantly more discontent with their lives than men in all three societies. Whereas 90 percent of the women had been employed in the host country, far fewer opportunities for paid work were available to them after going home (Gmelch and Gmelch 1995).

Roughly half of the male and female immigrants in my own study said they planned to return to Brazil, but unlike the findings on female migrants mentioned above, fewer women than men said they definitely intended to stay in the United States. The likely reason for this disparity is that most of the immigrant women I studied were single, while research suggests that it is *married* women who are most reluctant to go home to resume their traditional domestic lifestyles.

What about the other side of the equation? Why do immigrants return to Brazil, some even after a number of years in the United States? Here, too, the reasons are many. Some immigrants simply get fed up with the grinding working hours and the illusive goal of saving enough money for some ill-defined purpose back home. This is particularly true of older immigrants who came to the United States because a son or daughter had preceded them to this country (Martes 1995b). Some return to Brazil precisely because they *have* met their objective and have enough savings to buy a house or start a small business. These are the "target earners" mentioned earlier, immigrants who came to the

Some immigrants who are target earners eventually save enough money to buy a house in Brazil, such as this one in Governador Valadares.

United States with the sole intention of saving money to meet some specific goal in Brazil. For example, after two years in New York one immigrant I knew returned to Brazil with enough money to become a full-time university student. Other target earners were a married couple going home to make a downpayment on their dream house.

Once again, legal status may be a factor. As we have seen, obtaining a green card anchors some immigrants to the United States, but for others the opposite is true.[1] Although it seems paradoxical, receiving a green card can figure prominently in the decision to return to Brazil. One would think that having a green card and being able to work legally would be a strong incentive to stay in the United States, but the document actually provides still another option. Immigrants with green cards who return to Brazil and come to regret their decision can simply remigrate to the

1. One study of Central Americans in California found that legal status had virtually no effect on plans to stay in the United States or return home; 52% of legal immigrants and 47% of undocumented immigrants planned to remain in the United States (Chinchilla and Hamilton 1995).

United States within a year without any problem. Ironically, having a green card may make it easier to return home!

Of course, many immigrants are in a quandary about the decision to stay or to go. In my own study, about a third said they intended to stay in the United States and some 20 percent were undecided about the future. In these cases, there is often a condition attached to the return home: I will go back to Brazil if the economy there improves, if inflation remains low, if I ever save enough money to buy an apartment and a telephone[2], if good jobs open up for engineers, architects, teachers...Or conversely, I'll stay in New York if I get a green card, if I get a job here I like, if I marry my American girlfriend (or boyfriend). A conditional return is often a delayed return and the reasons for the delay can be situated in New York or in Brazil. For example, as a result of New York's economic recession of the late 1980s and early 1990s, some immigrants said that they kept delaying the return home because it had taken them longer to reach their goal of saving a particular sum of money. At the same time, others went back to Brazil when recession-induced unemployment reached 10 percent in New York, robbing them of their jobs in the city. In the mid-1990s, with inflation in Brazil seemingly under control for the first time in decades, Brazilians were more upbeat about the future of their country which presumably spurred many to return home.

How do all of these individual decisions translate into real numbers? How many Brazilians actually return home to stay? How many remain in the United States? And how many go back to Brazil "for good" only to turn around and come back to this country? While real numbers are illusive, I was able to relocate a little more than two-thirds of the one-hundred Brazilian immigrants in my study eighteen months after first interviewing them. Of these, 70 percent were still living in New York, 5 percent were residing elsewhere in the United States and one-quarter had returned to Brazil. In other words, about three-quarters of the immigrants I was able to locate were still residing in this country a year and a half after the original interview. It is possible that many, if not most, of those I could not find had returned to Brazil

---

2. Telephone lines are scarce in Brazil so a residential phone can cost $2,000 to $3,000.

and it is also possible that in the years to come still more immigrants will go back to Brazil to live. Finally, some of those now in the United States said they had actually returned to Brazil "for good" since the time of the interview, but had then remigrated to this country.

GOING HOME FOR GOOD?

Immigration in the jet age is often more circular than linear, a genuinely transnational process with waves of migrants moving back and forth across international borders, at times covering great distances. And, these movements may involve what I call yo-yo migration, the remigration of immigrants who have purportedly returned home "for good." The case of Huberto cited at the beginning of this chapter is an example of yo-yo migration. Recall that after several years in New York he bid the city farewell telling everyone he was going home to Brazil to live. Yet, within a couple of months he was planning his return to the United States. Despite the distance involved, I met several Brazilians in New York who had been traveling back and forth between Brazil and the United States for more than a decade. In other words, yo-yo migration may involve more than one "permanent" trip home. For example, over the ten years Paulo had lived in New York City he returned to Brazil three times "for good." Twice he stayed for more than a year before remigrating to the United States, the last time marrying and returning with his wife; they now have a New York-born child. Said one of his friends: "Everyday Paulo's going to Brazil to live and six months later—here he comes!" When I interviewed him Paulo insisted he was returning home "to try again." The last I heard he had gone back to Brazil "permanently," but his friend told me that Paulo plans to visit the United States once a year to maintain his status as a legal immigrant with a green card. After all, he never knows when it might come in handy!

Given the cost and distances involved, yo-yo migration between the United States and Brazil is more frequent than one would expect. Several times I was told of Brazilians who had gone back to Brazil for good, two, three, even four times, only to remigrate to the United States. In the words of political scientist Wayne Cornelius, these yo-yo migrants come closer to "commuting" than to "immigrating" (quoted in Grant 1981). Such returnees have been called "shuttle migrants" and "cultural commuters," people who move back and forth between home and host country and are never quite satisfied with their lives in either one. Studies suggest that some of these migrants are disillusioned when they return home and that homesickness in the host country is replaced by discontent with conditions in the homeland, a kind of reverse culture shock (Gmelch 1980; Bernard and Ashton-Vouyoucalos 1976; Bernard and Comitas 1978).

What explains this pattern of indecision, this bouncing back and forth between Brazil and the United States? Why did some immigrants who talked of little else but going home to Brazil, return there only to start planning their trip back to New York? In the late 1980s and early 1990s hyperinflation was the major catalyst for yo-yo migration. After returning home Brazilian immigrants soon found that the money saved in the United States provided little financial cushion in an economy with an inflation rate of 20 to 40 percent a month. But even after inflation was brought under control in the mid-1990s, the price of consumer goods in Brazil remained very high, particularly compared to the cost of similar items in the United States. People in the middle strata of Brazilian society had difficulty making ends meet as the cost of certain items—rent, medical care, school tuition and other services—soared above the overall rate of inflation with no general increase in salaries. This, in turn, led to sky high credit card debt and a rash of personal bankruptcies (Peluso and Goldberg 1995; O Globo 1995).

Returned migrants did not easily forget their relatively generous New York wages. As one Brazilian said of her compatriots:

"They're working full-time in Brazil and maybe earning $200 or $300 a month and they just can't forget that they were earning $300 or $400 *a week* in New York. They are always thinking about that, about how much more they used to earn there. It really bothers them and that's what spurs them to return to the United States."

The following scenario was played out time and again: returned migrants used their savings to buy an apartment in Brazil but then could not find a suitable job or, if they did get a job, soon learned how difficult it was to make ends meet on Brazilian wages. While they now had a nice place to live, that was not enough to anchor them permanently to their homeland. The lack of jobs that paid reasonably well was a major irritant that spurred remigration. Returnees with high levels of education and skill were likely to face the same economic barriers in Brazil—the dearth of decent paying jobs which made use of their talents—that had led them to migrate in the first place.

Still, going home to Brazil, regretting the decision and then returning to the United States is not as easy as one would think. For immigrants without green cards remigration can be a problem. I heard many tales of Brazilian immigrants who returned to Brazil with the intention of remaining there, changed their minds and then found it difficult or impossible to get tourist visas to get back into this country. Recall that would-be "tourists" suspected of being immigrants are routinely denied visas by American consular personnel. When this happened to one yo-yo migrant he was so anxious to return to New York that he paid $4000 for the documents—fake income tax returns and business ownership papers—needed to obtain a tourist visa.

Similar difficulties sometimes befall undocumented Brazilians who live in the United States and want to go back to Brazil to see relatives and friends or take care of business there. The following episode, while extreme, highlights the problem. João, an undocumented immigrant who had lived in New York for several years and owned a small flooring company in Queens, flew to Brazil when he received word that his elderly father was terminally ill. João's Brazilian wife, Gisele, and American-born daughter, Nara, remained behind in New York. When João returned to the United States he was stopped at the airport by American immigration officers, questioned and deported to Brazil because of evidence that he had previously overstayed his tourist visa. Gisele had no desire to return to Brazil to live and João, stuck in his hometown of Belo Horizonte, was so desperate to get back to his family and his business in the United States that he eventually did so by spending thousands of dollars to buy a passport with the coveted tourist visa stamped in it, both documents bearing someone else's name.

ARE THEY STILL COMING?

Are Brazilian immigrants still arriving in New York and other American cities in search of jobs, or has the improved economy back home slowed down or even halted the desire to seek one's fortune abroad? What impact did New York's economic downturn have on this migration stream? And, what is the perspective of Brazilian immigrants already in the United States on these issues? Have economic conditions in New York and Brazil influenced their decision to stay in this country or return home?

While I completed my formal research prior to the implementation of the Brazilian economic plan[3] that sharply curbed inflation, both my own anecdotal evidence and the findings of other researchers suggest that the improved economy neither stemmed the immigration flow nor caused Brazilians to return home en masse. Although exact figures do not exist, immigrants in Brazilian communities in New York, Boston and south Florida report that their compatriots are still arriving from Brazil. Researcher Cristina Martes, who interviewed Brazilians in Boston who came to the United States *after* the new economic plan went into effect, suggests that because would-be immigrants make travel plans months or years in advance, new arrivals had been planning to emigrate to this country well before inflation was brought under control in Brazil. Moreover, their lives had not been sufficiently affected by changes in the Brazilian economy to make them reconsider their long-term goal of seeking work in the United States (Martes 1995a).

Still, some observers of the immigrant scene insist that by the mid-1990s fewer Brazilians were emigrating to this country. Greater optimism about the Brazilian economy was only one factor in the slowdown, they say, and perhaps a minor one at that. The difficulty that Brazilians have had getting U.S. tourist visas was at least as important in dampening the transnational flow as was the purported improvement in the Brazilian economy.

Since the primary attraction of the United States for immigrants is jobs, it is the health of urban labor markets in this country—probably more than anything else—that affects the level of immigration and return. Evidence suggests that from the late 1980s on, Brazilians and other immigrants encountered fewer job opportunities in New York, Boston, and other cities and, as a result, some newly arrived Brazilian immigrants who could not find work promptly turned around and went home.

---

3. This plan was called "the *real* plan" after the new currency, the *real*, that was introduced as part of it.

Has New York's economic squeeze meant that fewer immigrants are arriving from Brazil in the first place? While there is no question that Brazilian immigrants are still coming to the city, a weaker job market probably has reduced the number somewhat. But, immigrants themselves disagreed on this point. While many in New York's Brazilian community were convinced that the city's economic downturn and subsequent rise in unemployment had caused a significant decline in Brazilian immigration, others argued that the flow of new arrivals from Brazil had not abated very much, if at all. "They're still coming, they're still coming," said a Baptist minister who serves New York's Brazilian community.

What about migration in the other direction? Has New York's economic slowdown influenced the decision of immigrants to return to Brazil? While many Brazilians did indeed leave the United States during my research, their numbers and motivation were unclear. Nevertheless, nearly everyone I talked with agreed that it had become harder for immigrants to find work and most thought that this was a major reason for the return home. The irony that some immigrants who went back to Brazil had been granted that much coveted document—a green card—allowing them to work legally in the United States, was not lost on their compatriots who remained behind in New York. "What good are documents, if you can't find a job?" one asked. "After all, if you can't get work in either place, isn't it better to live in your own country?"

HERE TO STAY

Many Brazilian immigrants have lived in New York since the initial immigration surge from their country in the mid-1980s. But at what point do these sojourners become settlers, people who see their future and the future of their children in their adopted land? How do Brazilians go from a mind set utterly focused on the return home to one that imagines a future in the United States? Changes in attitude and behavior are part of the passage from temporary resident to permanent settler. Subtle signs provide clues to this gradual shift and both work life and home life are affected by it. As more and more immigrants go through this process of transition, a community of sojourners is transformed into a community of settlers (Piore 1979).

Over time, immigrants become less willing to spend long days laboring away at jobs that go nowhere. They grow more reluctant to work extra hours or to hold down a second position. Working shorter hours, they earn less money, but they spend more of it on leisure. They eat out at restaurants and go to the movies more often or they are more likely to buy tickets to a concert or a sporting event. They may start to take trips outside the city, to Washington DC to see the nation's capital or to Florida to visit Disney World. Some even begin buying more warm clothes, deciding that a new winter coat is really not an extravagance if they are going to spend another year or two in the frosty clime of New York City.

Less time at work means more time is spent at home. Small cramped apartments with multiple roommates begin to grate on everyone's nerves. Brazilian immigrants start to think that having fewer people share an apartment might be worth the extra cost, while immigrant couples who rent out rooms may eventually decide that the additional money is just not worth the loss of privacy. As their stay in New York lengthens, many Brazilians become dissatisfied with their spartan home life and they begin spending money to fix up their apartments. While even the sparsely furnished dwellings of recent immigrants are often packed with stereo equipment, compact discs, televisions, VCRs, and state-of-the-art answering machines, it is understood that this electronic gear was actually purchased for the return home. But when immigrants begin renovating their apartments or buying major pieces of furniture or large appliances that can not be easily transported back to Brazil, it becomes evident that they no longer see their New York lives as "here today and gone tomorrow."

The process continues. Time passes, living conditions in New York slowly improve and the return home is put off for yet another year. Since immigrants are spending more on their lives in New York and saving less for the return to Brazil, their initial plan of going home with a certain sum of money in hand remains a distant goal. But, appearances to the contrary, most Brazilian immigrants *still* insist that they are planning to return home. Studies suggest that even after a number of their own deadlines for departure have passed, many immigrants cling to what has become a myth of return. Some, in fact, hold to an ideology of return no matter *how* long they have been in their adopted country (Castro

1985; Papapademetriou and DiMarzio 1986; Gmelch 1980). Perhaps this is why every immigrant interviewed for a magazine article about the Brazilian diaspora spoke of their ultimate goal: "When I'm old I want to return to Brazil and be buried there."

A Sea of Global Voyagers

Many Brazilian immigrants will become true transnationals. They will continue to live in the United States and they will see their lives and future as intimately tied to the fortunes and future of their new country. But they will not forsake Brazil. They will still go home on visits, they will maintain regular contact with family members who remain there, and they will never stop thinking of themselves as Brazilians. Then, too, as the quote above suggests, many are likely to retire to their native land.

The Brazilian transnational experience is just one variant of a global pattern. It is part of a world-wide phenomenon in which migrants from less industrialized nations travel what are often great distances to find work in the industrialized countries of North America, Europe, and Asia. Scholars of international migration have long sought to understand these global movements, some suggesting that the stream of peoples from newly industrializing to industrialized states is, in part, fostered by a desire for improved consumption and an enhanced style of life (Portes and Bach 1985). These aspirations are tied to increased levels of education in migrant-exporting nations along with greater media exposure to consumer patterns in advanced industrial states. This helps explain why international migrants, like those from Brazil, often do not come from the poorest nations or from the most impoverished regions of their own nations.

International migration also can help diffuse worrisome social and economic problems within migrant-sending states. For example, in many Latin American and other newly industrializing economies, capital-intensive industrial and agricultural development has created labor surpluses. Labor surpluses stimulate emigration because they increase unemployment and depress wages and living standards, including, in some cases, living standards of the middle class. This is one reason why in recent years middle-class migrants from the industrializing world have become part of these global movements. The departure of well-educated migrants, in turn, helps alleviate the dilemma of the "over-qualified" in many migrant-sending nations. As in the case of Brazil, the dilemma arises when large numbers of professionals are trained, but even though their skills are needed at home, not enough jobs are available at wages they deem adequate given their many years of schooling. Labor market realities in some developing nations, then, have stymied expectations of social mobility for a segment of their well-educated and highly trained citizenry. International migration diffuses the situation, in part, by sending many of the over-qualified abroad.

The global travel of this educated "surplus" as well as of international migrants in general serves yet another important function. Given the low wages and under-employment that plague many industrializing nations, the remittance money that migrants send from their jobs abroad helps subsidize family members back home. By cushioning their families economically, migrants' remittances dissipate the political unrest that might arise among a disgruntled populace beset by low wages, falling living standards and limited economic opportunities.

A few figures indicate just how important remittances are to the economies of some industrializing nations. Estimates suggest that from $4 billion to $6 billion annually is transferred back to Mexico by relatives in the United States, while fully one-third of the income of the Dominican Republic comes from the dollars immigrants send home. Even in Brazil, the world's eighth largest economy, the estimated 1.5 million Brazilians living abroad—a mere one percent of the Brazilian population—are thought to have remitted the impressive sum of 4 billion dollars in 1996 alone (Case 1996; Fisher 1996; Klintowitz 1996:26)!

The benefits of international migration, however, do not flow in only one direction. Despite the anti-immigrant sentiment that is a part of contemporary discourse in the industrial world, the truth is that host nations also gain from these global currents. After all, the industrial nations that are the objects of transnational migrants' desire are in the enviable position of having a huge supply of cheap labor clamoring to fill jobs most citizens of their own lands reject out of hand (Piore 1979, 1986). And, as we have seen, advanced industrial countries are now even attracting well-educated, highly motivated immigrants—like middle class Brazilians—for what are very menial jobs. Through legislation and selective enforcement of immigration laws, moreover, these nations can both generate a useful supply of inexpensive, powerless labor and partially regulate its conditions of entry.

Global voyagers are beneficial to advanced industrialized nations not only for the relatively low cost of their labor, but for their transience. Initially, at least, most international migrants view their stay abroad as temporary, often lasting only enough time to save money for the return home. It is this built-in impermanence that melds so neatly with the type of work that most immigrants do. International migrants are overwhelmingly employed in jobs with low wages, little job security, few or no benefits, low prestige, and little or no opportunity for advancement. Because of their many undesirable features, finding native-born workers to fill these jobs is difficult or impossible. But international migrants who see themselves as here today and gone tomorrow are more sanguine about the lack of career prospects and other liabilities of such work.

The benefits of transnational migration to the industrialized world are substantial. It provides a mass of low cost, often well-educated workers, who are willing, even eager, to take a variety of jobs that otherwise might go unfilled. And, at the same time, international migration relieves some of the economic and political pressures that might otherwise threaten the stability of many newly industrializing nations.

Postscript

In October 1996 the newly elected president of the Dominican Republic returned to New York City where he had grown up, the son of immigrants. His advice to fellow Dominicans might apply to transnational migrants of any nationality:

> "If you, young mother, or you, elderly gentleman, or you, young student, feel the need to adopt the nationality of the United States...do not feel tormented by this. Do it with a peaceful conscience, for you will continue being Dominicans, and we will welcome you as such when you set foot on the soil of our republic" (quoted in Rohter 1996).

References

Adelson, Andrea
   1996   "U.S. Set to Link 2 Retailers to Sweatshop-Made Goods."
           New York Times, May 20, p. D2.

Apsan, Moises
   1995   "Os Conselheiros de Imigração." *The Brasilians,* May, p. 6.

Araujo, Ledice
   1995   "Serviços: Altas de Até 200% São Difíceis de Engolir." *O
           Globo,* July 1, p. 4.

Badgley, Ruey T.
   1994   "Brazucas in Beantown: The Dynamics of Brazilian Ethnicity
           in Boston." Senior Honors Thesis in Anthropology, Connect-
           icut College, New London, Connecticut.

Bailey, Thomas R.
   1987   *Immigrant and Native Workers: Contrasts and Competition.*
           Boulder: Westview Press.

Basch, Linda, Nina Glick Schiller and Cristina Szanton Blanc
   1994   *Nations Unbound: Transnational Projects, Postcolonial Predica-
           ments, and Deterritorialized Nation-States.* Langhorne, Pa:
           Gordon and Breach.

Bean, Frank D., Barry Edmonston, and Jeffery S. Passel, eds.
   1990   *Undocumented Migration to the United States: IRCA and the
           Experience of the 1980's.* Santa Monica: The Rand Corporation
           and Washington, D.C.: The Urban Institute.

Bernard, H. Russell
   1994   *Research Methods in Anthropology: Qualitative and Quantitative
           Approaches,* 2nd edition. Newbury Park, CA: Sage.

Bernard, H. Russell and Sandy Ashton-Vouyoucalos
1976 "Return Migration to Greece." *Journal of the Steward Anthropological Society* 8(1): 31–52.

Bernard, H. Russell and Lambros Comitas
1978 "Greek Return Migration." *Current Anthropology* 19(3): 658–659.

Bonacich, Edna and John Modell
1980 *The Economic Basis of Ethnic Solidarity: Small Business in the Japanese-American Community.* Berkeley: University of California Press.

Brazilian Voice
1995 "Empresários brasileiros temerosos com as blitz da imigração." April 28–May 4.

Brenner, Leslie
1991 "The New New York." *New York Woman,* April, pp. 68–81.

Briggs, Vernon M., Jr. and Stephen Moore
1994 *Still An Open Door? U.S. Immigration Policy and the American Economy.* Washington, DC: The American University Press.

Brimelow, Peter
1995 *Alien Nation: Common Sense About America's Immigration Disaster.* New York: Random House.

Brooke, James
1993 "In Brazil Wild Ways to Counter Wild Inflation." *New York Times,* July 25, p. 11
1994 "Economy Dampens Ardor of Brazilians." *New York Times,* January 5, C11.
1994 "Brazilians Get Serious on Inflation and Deficit." *New York Times,* March 3, p. D2

Buchanan, Susan H.
1979 "Haitian Women in New York City." *Migration Today,* VII (4): 19–25, 39.

Bustos, Sergio R.
1995 "South Florida Becomes Haven for Brazilians." *Fort Lauderdale Sun Sentinel,* February 12, pp. 1, 11.

Butcher, Kristin F. and David Card
1991 "Immigration and Wages: Evidence from the 1980s." *Economic Impact of Immigration* 81(2): 292–96.

Case, Brendan M.
1996   "Cashing in on Immigration." *New York Times,* September 14, pp. 17–18.

Castro, Mary Garcia
1985   "Work Versus Life: Colombian Women in New York." In *Women and Change in Latin America.* June Nash and Helen Safa, eds. South Hadley, Mass.: Bergin & Garvey, pp. 231–259.

Chavez, Leo R.
1988   "Settlers and Sojourners: The Case of Mexicans in the United States." *Human Organization* 47(2): 95–107.
1989   "Households, Migration and Settlement: A Comparison of Undocumented Mexicans and Central Americans in the United States." Paper presented at the 88th annual meetings of the American Anthropological Association,Washington, D.C.

Cheever, Susan
1995   "The Nanny Track." *The New Yorker,* March 6, pp. 84–95.

Chigusa, Charles Tetsuo, ed.
1994   *A Quebra dos Mitos: O Fenômeno Dekassegui Através de Relatos Pessoais.* Mizuhiki, Japan: IPC Produção & Consultoria.

Chinchilla, Norma Stoltz and Nora Hamilton
1995   "Sojourners, Settlers or Returnees: Factors in Decisions of Central Americans to Remain or Return." Paper presented at the 19th International Congress of the Latin American Studies Association, Washington, DC.

Colen, Shellee
1990   "'Housekeeping for the Green Card: West Indian Household Workers, the State, and Stratified Reproduction in New York." In *At Work in Homes: Household Workers in World Perspective.* Roger Sanjek and Shellee Colen, eds., AES Monograph Series, Washington D.C., pp. 89–118.

Cornelius, Wayne A.
1982   "Interviewing Undocumented Immigrants: Methodological Reflections Based on Fieldwork in Mexico and the U.S. *International Migration Review* 16(2): 378–411.

Corrêa, Marcos Sá
1994   "O Brasil Se Expande." *Veja,* September 7, pp. 70–77.

Cristina, Léa
1995 "Brasil Supera EUA Nos Preços." *O Globo,* July 1, p. 4.

Da Matta, Roberto
1991 *Carnivals, Rogues, and Heroes, An Interpretation of the Brazilian Dilemma.* John Drury, trans. Notre Dame, IN: University of Notre Dame Press.

De Souza, Okky
1996 "Por Baixo do Pano." *Veja,* April 10, pp. 60–62.

Dugger, Celia W.
1996 "A Tattered Crackdown on Illegal Workers." *New York Times,* June 3, pp. 1, B6.

Dunn, Ashley
1995 "Greeted at Nation's Front Door, Many Visitors Stay on Illegally." *New York Times,* January 3, pp. 1, B2.

Ehrlich, Claudia
1989 "Beyond Black and White: A Perspective on Racial Attitudes of Paulistas in São Paulo and New York." Senior Project, Division of Social Studies, Bard College, Annandale-on-Hudson, New York.
1990 "Stereotypes of Racial Conflict."*Link* 10 (November):8–9.

Espenshade, Thomas J.
1995 "Unauthorized Immigration to the United States." *Annual Review of Sociology,* Vol. 21.

Feldman-Bianco, Bela
1992 "Multiple Layers of Time and Space: The Construction of Class, Ethnicity and Nationalism Among Portuguese Immigrants." In *Towards a Transnational Perspective on Migration: Race, Class, Ethnicity and Nationalism Reconsidered.* Glick Schiller, Nina, Linda Basch and Cristina Blanc Szanton, eds. Volume 645, Annals of the New York Academy of Sciences, New York, pp. 145–174.

Firestone, David
1996 "Giuliani Planning to Sue Over U.S. Welfare Provision." *New York Times,* September, 12, p. 14.

Fisher, Ian
1996 "Dominican Leader's Triumphant Tour." *New York Times,* October 5, p. 27.

Fix, Michael and Jeffrey S. Passel
1994 *Immigration and Immigrants: Setting the Record Straight.* Washington, DC: The Urban Institute.

Foner, Nancy
1986   "Sex Roles and Sensibilities: Jamaican Women in New York and London." In *International Migration: The Female Experience*. Rita J. Simon and Caroline B. Brettell, eds., Totowa, NJ: Rowman & Allanheld, pp. 133–151.

Freedman, Marcia
1983   "The Labor Market for Immigrants in New York City." *New York Affairs* 7: 94–110.

Freyre, Gilberto
1964   *The Masters and the Slaves*. rev. and abridged 2nd edition, New York: Borzoi.

Fundação Instituto Brasileiro de Geografia e Estatística
1994   "Cor da População: Síntese de Indicadores 1982/1990." Rio de Janeiro: Instituto Brasileiro de Geografia e Estatística.

Gmelch, George
1980   "Return Migration." *Annual Review of Anthropology* 9: 135–159. Palo Alto, Ca.: Annual Reviews.

Gmelch, George and Sharon Bohn Gmelch
1995   "Gender and Migration: The Readjustment of Women Migrants in Barbados, Ireland, and Newfoundland." *Human Organization* 54(4): 470–73.

Gold, Steven J.
1995   *From the Workers' State to the Golden State: Jews from the Former Soviet Union in California*. Boston: Allyn & Bacon.

Golden, Tim
1991   "Mexicans Head North Despite Job Rules." *New York Times*, December 13, pp. 1, 28.

Gonzalez, David
1992   "What's the Problem with 'Hispanic'? Just Ask a 'Latino.'" *New York Times*, November, 15, section 4, p. 6.

Grant, Geraldine
1981   *New Immigrants and Ethnicity: A Preliminary Research Report on Immigrants in Queens*. New York: Queens College Ethnic Studies Project.

Grasmuck, Sherri and Patricia R. Pessar
1992   *Between Two Islands: Dominican International Migration*. Berkeley: University of California Press.

Haines, David
1986 "Vietnamese Refugee Women in the U.S. Labor Force: Conti-
      nuity or Change?" In *International Migration: The Female
      Experience.* Rita J. Simon and Caroline B. Brettell, eds.,
      Totowa, NJ: Rowman & Allanheld, pp. 62–75.

Hondagneu-Sotelo, Pierrette
1994 *Gendered Transitions: Mexican Experiences of Immigration.* Ber-
      keley: University of California Press.

Hunt, George
1996 "Raids and Arrests." *America,* July 20, p. 3

Johnston, David Cay
1995 "The Servant Class Is at the Counter." *New York Times,*
      August 27, section 4, pp. 1, 4.

Kilborn, Peter T.
1993 "Law Failed to Stem Illegal Immigration, Panel Says." *New
      York Times,* February 11, p. 16.

Klintowitz, Jaime
1996 "Nossa Gente Lá Fora." *Veja,* April 3, pp. 26–29.

Kottak, Conrad Phillip
1990 *Prime Time Society: An Anthropological Analysis of Television
      and Culture.* Belmont, Ca.: Wadsworth.

Kwong, Peter
1994 "The Wages of Fear: Undocumented and Unwanted,
      Fuzhounese Immigrants are Changing the Face of China-
      town." *Village Voice,* April 26, pp. 25–29.

Lee, Felicia R.
1995 "Slaying Shocks Usually Upbeat Brazilians." *New York Times,*
      September 21, pp. B1, B3.

Linger, Daniel T.
1995 "Brazilians in Toyota City: An Ethnographic Field Report."
      Prepared for the Toyota International Association. Universi-
      ty of California, Santa Cruz. mimeo.

Longman, Jere
1994 "1 Team, but 150 Million Coaches." *New York Times,* May 10,
      p. B15.

Lucena, Eliana
1996 "Estudo Aponta Emigração de um Milhão." *Jornal do Brasil,*
      March 29.

Mahler, Sarah J.
1995   *American Dreaming: Immigrant Life on the Margins.* Princeton: Princeton University Press.

Margolis, Mac
1994   "Brazil and the United States, Stay Away." *The Economist,* October 29, pp. 48, 50.

Margolis, Maxine L.
1984   *Mothers and Such: Views of American Women and Why They Changed.* Berkeley: University of California Press.
1989   "A New Ingredient in the 'Melting Pot': Brazilians in New York City." *City & Society* 3(2): 179–87.
1990   An American in Governador Valadares. *The Brasilians* 199, September, p. 4.
1994   *Little Brazil: An Ethnography of Brazilian Immigrants in New York City.* Princeton: Princeton University Press.
1995a "Brazilians and the 1990 United States Census: Immigrants, Ethnicity and the Undercount." *Human Organization* 54(1): 52–59.
1995b "Transnationalism and Popular Culture: The Case of Brazilian Immigrants in the United States." *Journal of Popular Culture* 29(1): 29–41.

Mariz, Cecilia Loreto
1994   *Coping with Poverty: Pentecostals and Christian Base Communities in Brazil,* Philadelphia: Temple University Press.

Martes, Ana Cristina Braga
1995a "Brazilian Immigrants in the United States." Research proposal. mimeo.
1995b "Relatório Capes/Fulbright." Cambridge. mimeo
1996   "Solidariedade e Competição: Acesso ao Mercado de Trabalho e Atuação das Igrejas entre os Imigrantes Brasileiros na Área de Boston." mimeo.

Massey, Douglas S.
1988   "Economic Development and International Migration in Comparative Perspective." *Population and Development Review* 14(3): 383–411.

Miller, Charlotte I.
1979   "The Function of Middle-Class Extended Family Networks in Brazilian Urban Society." In *Brazil: Anthropological Perspectives.* Maxine L. Margolis and William E. Carter, eds. New York: Columbia University Press. pp. 305–316.

Mishel, Lawrence and Jared Bernstein
  1996 "The State of Working America 1996–97." Washington, D.C.:
        Economic Policy Institute.

Moura, Germana Costa and Léa Cristina
  1996 "Três Brasis Dentro de um Só País." *O Globo,* June 1, p. 21.

Mydans, Seth
  1991 "More Mexicans Come to U.S. to Stay." *New York Times,* Jan-
        uary 21, p. 14.

Neto, João Sorima and Ernesto Bernardes
  1996 "A Miami do Brasil." *Veja,* July 17, pp. 50–65.

New York Times
  1994 "Brazilians Celebrate on the Streets of Manhattan." July 18,
        p. C4.

News from Brazil
  1990 "Lost Angels." No. 41 (December), Los Angeles.

O'Dougherty, Maureen
  1995 "International Bargain Shopping: Consumption and Brazil-
        ian Middle Class Identity in the 1990s." Paper presented at
        the 19th International Congress of the Latin American Stud-
        ies Association, Washington, DC.

O Globo
  1995 "Classe Média Passou Logo da Euforia à Inadimplência."
        July 1, p. 4.

Osava, Mario
  1996 "Brazil: Minimum Salary in the Hands of the Legal System."
        InterPress Service.

Papademetriou, Demetrios G. and Nicholas DiMarzio
  1986 *Undocumented Aliens in the New York Metropolitan Area.* New
        York: Center for Migration Studies.

Peluso, Luciana and Simone Goldberg
  1995 "Heróis da Sobrevivência." *Isto É,* December 7, pp. 124–129.

Pessar, Patricia R.
  1985 "When the Birds of Passage Want to Roost: An Exploration of
        the Role of Gender in Dominican Settlement in the U.S." In
        Women and Change in Latin America. June Nash and Helen I.
        Safa, eds. South Hadley, Mass.: Bergin & Harvey, pp. 273–94.
  1995 "The Elusive Enclave: Ethnicity, Class, and Nationality
        among Latino Entrepreneurs in Greater Washington, D.C."
        Human Organization 54 (4): 383–92.

Piore, Michael J.
  1979 *Birds of Passage: Migrant Labor and Industrial Societies.* New York: Cambridge.
  1986 "The Shifting Grounds for Migration." *Annals of the American Academy of Political and Social Science* 485: 23–33.

Portes, Alejandro and Robert L. Bach
  1985 *Latin Journey: Cuban and Mexican Immigrants in the United States.* Berkeley: University of California Press.

Repak, Terry A.
  1995 *Waiting on Washington: Central American Workers in the Nation's Capital.* Philadelphia: Temple University Press.

Rohter, Larry
  1996 "Despite Tougher Laws, U.S. Lures Dominicans." *New York Times,* October 12, p. 7.

Safa, Helen I.
  1995 "Economic Restructuring and Gender Subordination." *Latin American Perspectives* 22(2): 33–51.

Sassen-Koob, Saskia
  1986 "New York City: Economic Restructuring and Immigration." *Development and Change* 17: 85–119.

Schemo, Diana Jean
  1996 "Brazil's Economic Samba." *New York Times,* September 7, pp. 35, 37.

Schmitt, Eric
  1996 "Giuliani Criticizes G. O. P. and Dole on Immigration." *New York Times,* June 7, p. B3.

Simon, Rita J. and Margo Corona DeLey
  1986 "Undocumented Mexican Women: Their Work and Personal Experiences." In *International Migration: The Female Experience.* Rita J. Simon and Caroline B. Brettell, eds., Totowa, NJ: Rowman & Allanheld, pp. 113–132.

Sims, Calvin
  1995 "The South American Art of Name-Calling." *New York Times,* July 30, p. E4.

Sontag, Deborah
  1993 "Emigres in New York: Work Off the Books." *New York Times,* June 13, pp. 1, 42.
  1994 "U.S. Arrests 3 in Immigration Marriage Fraud." *New York Times,* July 22,pp. 1, B2.

Suárez-Orozco, Carola and Marcelo Suárez-Orozco
1995   "Migration: Generational Discontinuities and the Making of Latino Identitities." In *Ethnic Identity: Creation, Conflict and Accomodation*. Lola Romanucci-Ross and George DeVos, eds. Walnut Creek, Ca: Altamira Press, pp. 321–347.

Suro, Roberto
1990   "Traffic in Fake Documents is Blamed as Illegal Immigration Rises Anew." *New York Times*, November 26, p. 9.

Thurow, Lester
1995   "Why Their World Might Crumble. *New York Times Magazine*, November 19, pp. 78–79.

United States Immigration and Naturalization Service
1996   *1994 Statistical Yearbook*. Washington, D.C.: U.S. Government Printing Office.

Usdansky, Margaret L.
1993   "Immigrants' Status: Many Factors in the Mix." *USA Today*, November 6, p. 10A.

Veja
1995a "Os Preços Muito Loucos da Era do Real." July 19, pp. 18–24.
1995b "Multinacional da Fé." April 19, pp. 92–94.

Wagley, Charles
1971   *Introduction to Brazil*. 2nd edition. New York: Columbia University Press.

Waldinger, Roger
1989   "Immigration and Urban Change." *Annual Review of Sociology*, Vol 15. Palo Alto: Annual Reviews, pp. 211–232.
1993   *Black/Immigrant Competition Re-assessed: New Evidence from Los Angeles*. Los Angeles: UCLA, Department of Sociology.
1996   *Still the Promised City? New Immigrants and African-Americans in Post-Industrial New York*. Cambridge: Harvard University Press.

Warren, Robert
1995   "Estimates of the Unauthorized Immigrant Population Residing in the United States by Country of Origin and State of Residence, October 1992." Washington DC: INS Statistical Division. April 29.

Wright, Robert
1995   "Who's Really to Blame?" *Time Magazine*, November 6.

Yoon, In-Jin
  1991   "The Changing Significance of Ethnic and Class Resources in Immigrant Businesses: The Case of Korean Immigrant Business in Chicago." *International Migration Review* 25(2):120–130.

Zentgraf, Kristine
  1995   "Household Composition, Decision to Settle and the Changing Political Economic Context: Central Americans in Los Angeles." Paper presented at the 19th International Congress of the Latin American Studies Association, Washington, DC.